THE PROFESSOR'S ATTITUDE
AND PERFORMANCE

Submitted as a dissertation to the Graduate School, Northwestern University, in partial fulfillment of the requirements for the degree of Doctor of Philosophy, Field of Organizational Behavior, 1975.

RAFAEL COLON CORA

THE PROFESSOR'S ATTITUDE
AND PERFORMANCE

EDITORIAL UNIVERSITARIA
UNIVERSIDAD DE PUERTO RICO
RIO PIEDRAS
1981

Primera edición, 1981

Catalogación de la Biblioteca del Congreso
Library of Congress Cataloging in Publication Data

Colón Cora, Rafael, 1945-

The professor's attitude and performance.

Originally presented as the author's thesis, Northwestern University, 1975, under title: A social psychological analysis of the determinants of faculty performance in the universities of Puerto Rico.

Bibliography: p.
Includes index.

1. College teachers—Puerto Rico. 2. College teachers, Rating of. I. Title.

LB2333.C58   1978   378.1'22   78-12813
ISBN 0-8477-2450-6

Depósito Legal: B. 32.303 - 1981

Printed in Spain

Editorial Universitaria. Apartado de Correos X
Estación de la Universidad de Puerto Rico
Río Piedras, Puerto Rico 00931

TABLE OF CONTENTS

LIST OF TABLES

For my Mother, Luisa, Aida,
Pura, Doris, Checo and Gil.

ACKNOWLEDGMENTS

I am indebted to Professor Joseph Moag for serving as chairman of my doctoral committee, for his advice and guidance throughout my graduate program and for his effort in helping me to complete this work. Without his participation I could not have finished this dissertation. I am especially appreciative of Dr. Robert Duncan, Dr. Charles Thompson, and Dr. Edward P. T. Watson for serving on my doctoral committee and for their assistance.

Armando Triana, Luis Mario Salces, Harold Welch, Mike Keely, Liu Shvei-Shen, and all the members of the Department of Organizational Behavior also deserve acknowledgments for their assistance and helpful comments about this work.

Acknowledgments are gratefully accorded to the Graduate School of Business Administration of the University of Puerto Rico and the Graduate School of Northwestern University for financial support throughout my doctoral program. I should like to recognize particularly the interest of Dr. Carlos Toro and Professor Georgina Falú in obtaining financial support for this thesis.

Gratitude is expressed to all the professors of the universities of Puerto Rico who participated as respondents in this study. Dr. Pedro González Ramos, President of the Colegio Universitario Sagrado Corazón, Dr. Rafael Pietri Oms, Chancellor of the University of Puerto Rico at Mayagüez, Dr. Ismael Rodríguez Bou, Chancellor of the University of Puerto Rico at Rio Piedras, Dr. Herman Sulsona, Chancellor of the Administration of Community Colleges of the University of Puerto Rico, Professor Federico Modesto, Chancellor of the Puerto Rico Junior College, Professor Genaro Beltrán, professor of the University of Puerto Rico at Cayey, Professor Orlando R. O'Neill, Director of the Junior College at Colegio Universitario Sagrado Corazón, and Professor José D. Cotte, professor in the Humacao Regional College, deserve my gratitude for helping me in this study. They allowed and encouraged me to collect the data used in this dissertation.

A grateful note of appreciation must go to Susan Mohrman, Barbara Yocum, and Pat Millow for the part they took in the editing of this work.

PREFACE

This book deals with a topic that is pertinent both to social scientists concerned with behavior in the work setting and to those individuals who occupy positions in the management of universities and other organizations. The topic concerns the social psychological determinants of the professor's performance.

We used the path-goal theory of work motivation in order to predict the behavior of faculty at the university. The study uses Porter and Lawler's elaboration of the path-goal model, adapted where necessary to accomodate the university setting.

It was further necessary to introduce role theory as a complement to Porter and Lawler's model so as to refine their variable of role perception. Because of this, this study is also a study of the effects of the discrepancy between a professor's and a chairman's perceptions of the professor's role.

The study had three basic findings. First, the path-goal model does predict, although weakly, the professor's effort on his job. Second, role discrepancy does predict rather strongly the professor's evaluation of his own performance, but does not predict as had been expected the chairman's evaluation of performance.

A further finding of interest was the relationship between the professor's and the chairman's perception of the professor's role. The study found, in particular, that there was a very strong correlation between role discrepancy and both the influence of people outside the university and the influence of colleagues.

Third, the study found, as expected, that the organizational setting, especially climate variables, had a positive relationship with the professor's reported overall job satisfaction and a strong and negative relationship with felt deficiencies in the amount of rewards he receives.

A less definite relationship was found between effort and performance evaluations and organizational setting variables.

May, 1978   Rafael Colón Cora

I. INTRODUCTION

It is generally accepted that if any organization is to function effectively it needs to exercise influence over the behavior of its employees. Consequently, organizations which employ large numbers of professionals—who value and obtain a great deal of freedom from organizational constraints—may be faced with problems of influencing their behavior, of motivating them in order to attain its (organizational) goals.

The university would fit the description presented above. One of the major problems confronting academic institutions is the evaluation of and influence over faculty performance. Usually the faculty members perceive that they have enough ability and knowledge and it is not necessary to evaluate their performance. Many of the faculty's members are reluctant to be evaluated. As a matter of fact, they consider that the evaluation is degrading. Furthermore, many faculty members do not accept the normal aproaches to influence found in various types of organizations.

However, we consider that the university, as any organization, needs to evaluate and influence the performance of its professors. Otherwise the university would not have any means to determine how well it is performing its role in society or of achieving it.

The role of the university is fundamental in any country; however, in the underdeveloped countries its role is critical, because the university has the responsibility to create, foster, and evaluate the fundamental changes in the country. The university must be the leader of any social change and must foster any scientific movement toward the development of the country.

However, the university cannot accomplish its role if it does not have a means to predict the behavior of its professors and to motivate them toward the attainment of the university's goals.

The purpose of this study is to examine a motivational model that seems useful in accomplishing this objective: to predict and explain the professor's work behavior at the university.

Furthermore, since there is some question as to the efficacy of various behavioral theories of work behavior as to their applications to professionals (and more specifically to university professors) this study attempts to contribute to this issue of behavioral theory.

It attempts to evaluate an Expectancy Model of Motivation, to test aspects of the model which have not been sufficiently tested, to improve the measures of its variables, and to consider this model jointly with organizational variables to determine their effect upon the outcome of the model.

The research site is the universities of Puerto Rico. The fact that this study is conducted in a different culture and with professionals, adds additional interest to it. The motivational model that we are going to evaluate has never been tested in a Latin American culture.

II. THEORY AND HYPOTHESES

BACKGROUND TO CURRENT RESEARCH

The search for adequate explanations and predictions of varying levels of productivity observed among organizational members has been a major concern to psychologists in industrial psychology. Following Mayo's Hawthorne experiments [1] in the 1920s, the search has broadened to include job satisfaction differences. And, in more recent years, it has been extended further to encompass the question of the correlation and link between productivity and satisfaction. Increasingly, this three-fold interest has led to research in numerous empirical settings, and still continues to be a major concern in much current research (Georgopoulos, 1971; Vroom, 1964; Herzberg et al., 1959; Brayfield and Crockett, 1955, among others).

Brayfield and Crockett (1955) after an extensive review of the literature concluded "...it appears that there is little evidence in the available literature that employee attitudes of the type usually measured in a morale survey bear any simple—or for that matter, appreciable—relationship to performance on the job." [2]

But in 1957 Herzberg et al.[3] published a comprehensive review of research concerned with the area of job attitudes in which they displayed a different viewpoint than did Brayfield and Crockett. Listing well over 1,000 references, the examined job attitude studies under the various headings of job dissatisfaction, effects of attitudes, factor related job attitudes, supervision of job attitudes,

---

1. E. Mayo, *The Human Problems of an Industrial Civilization*, New York, MacMillan Co., 1933.

2. A. Brayfield and W. Crockett, «Employee Attitudes and Employee Performance,» *Psychological Bulletin*, 1955, 55, pp. 396-424.

3. F. Herzberg et al., *The Motivation to Work*, New York, John Wiley & Son, Inc., 1959.

vocational selection and job attitudes, and mental health in industry.

They concluded that positive job attitudes are a tremendous asset to industry, a contention supported by much of the experimental evidence available in the years they did the research. In support of this statement they pointed to evidence of the relation of attitudes to turnover, absenteeism and accidents.

Herzberg, et al.'s conclusions raised many question among the specialists in the field. Since 1959 much of the research in the area of job satisfaction has been concerned with the exploration of possible differences in the dimensionality of job satisfaction and job dissatisfaction, as well as with the generality of the results of the Herzberg et al. study (Wernimont, 1964, among others).

But with all the studies that analyzed the relation between productivity and satisfaction, it seems that they did not represent an adequate explanation of the different levels of productivity observed among organizational members.

For example, Georgopoulos said "the problem of the relationship between productivity and satisfaction remained relatively issue-free until the well-known review of the research literature on attitudes, satisfaction, and performance by Brayfield and Crockett. Their review "...[found that] although many studies found productivity and satisfaction to correlate positively, others had found no significant relationship between the two, and some had found a negative instead of the presumed positive relationship." [4]

In a recent book Lawler (1973) raised a strong critique to the research on the relationship between productivity and satisfaction. He said "that the research on job satisfaction has typically been atheoretical and has not tested for causal relationships. Since the research has not been guided by theory a vast array of unorganized virtually uninterpretable facts have been unearthed." [5]

Due to present limitations, the research on job satisfaction does not provide enough understanding to shed light over the problem of the determinants of productivity. Owing to the lack of a theory stating causal relationships—among other limitations—this research has consistently looked simply for relationships among variables.

---

4. B. Georgopoulos, «Individual Performance and Job Satisfaction Differences Explained with Instrumentality Theory and Expectancy Models as a Function of Path-Goal Relationships.» Reprinted from *Progress and Clinical Psychology*, Orune & Stratton, Inc., 1971, p. 57.

5. E. Lawler, *Motivation in Work Organizations*, California, Brooks/Cole Publishing Company, 1973.

Probably a great deal is known about what factors are related to satisfaction, but very little is known about the causal basis for the relationship. This is a serious problem when one attempts to base change efforts on this research.

We can conclude that there is a *necessity to continue doing research in order to improve our knowledge about productivity and satisfaction.* Like other theories and models in organizational behavior, more reseach is needed because our understanding of individual performance and job satisfaction, and their relationship, is still rather inadequate, and since these variables still focus the consciousness of workers, managers and researchers, their relationships are worth pursuing.

THE PATH-GOAL MODEL OF WORK BEHAVIOR

One of the most persistent approaches to the understanding of worker performance and worker satisfaction is the path-goal model of behavior, especially the instrumentality-expectancy version of this model. This chapter will (1) examine the research which has been done in support of this model; (2) discuss the strengths and limitations of this model as discussed in the literature; (3) discuss organizational variables, as these have been hypothesized as modifying explanations of the path-goal model; (4) discuss my own hypothesis of the relationship between and salience of variables in the path-goal model and organizational contingencies, both as these relate to various theories of behavior and to the specific contingencies of university life; and, finally, (5) set forth the working hypothesis underlying the data gathered for this study.

As Georgopoulos has said, the path-goal model of work behavior seeks to explain individual variability in performance and satisfaction on the assumption that work behavior is motivated and goal-directed.[6] According to him much of the variance in performance can be demonstrably related to, and accounted for by, motivational variability concerning work-relevant individual goals. He based his conclusion on the assumption that since job satisfaction constitutes one of the principal personal goals pursued by organization members, and work performance constitutes one of the main paths leading to job satisfaction, it too can be accounted for on the same basis.

---

6. Basil Georgopoulos, *op. cit.,* p. 52.

Georgopoulos considered that two major explanatory concepts are commonly employed by path-goal formulation in order to explain the relationship of satisfaction and performance: the concept of expectancy, representing the notion of subjective expectation or psychological probability; and the concept of value, representing the notion of preference, attractiveness, or valence.

In other words, the behavior of the individual could be explained through his expectations that his job performance will lead him to the attainment of an attractive goal. Furthermore, Georgopoulos assumed that job satisfaction is a personal goal pursued by organizational members, and that individual performance is an instrument in obtaining this goal.

According to him, this basic formulation is consistent with the motivational theory elaborated by Atkinson.[7] This theory said that behavior is a multiplicative function of motivational disposition, incentive, expectancy, and habit. It also stated that the psychological utility of an activity is the product of interaction between the motivational disposition of the individual and available incentive.

However, this approach does not explain how performance will lead to job satisfaction nor does it theorize as to whether this relationship could be moderated or affected by other variables or conditions in the organization. It furthermore, assumes that job satisfaction is a goal that every member in the organization must pursue, but does not present any support for this assumption. Nevertheless, the explanation is useful in summarizing what has been done in the field about the relationship between satisfaction and performance.

These formulations have been elaborated and extended in several directions by the different path-goal models of work behavior. One of the earliest was the Georgopoulos, Mahoney, and Jones model.[8] They proposed that individual productivity is a function of the level of need of the individual for specific goals and of his level of freedom from constraining factors, both personal and situational, as well as of his path-goal perception. These researchers assumed that people in any social situation tend to pursue among available goals those which promise to satisfy their needs. They proposed that if people perceive their productivity as an instrument to obtain a particular goal that will fulfill their need they

---

7. This theory was presented by J. W. Atkinson in his book, *An Introduction to Motivation*, Princeton, Van Nostrand, 1964.

8. Basil Georgopoulos *et al.* «A Path-Goal Approach to Productivity,» *Journal of Applied Psychology*, 1957, *41*, pp. 345-353.

will increase their productivity. "If a worker sees high productivity as a path leading to the attainment of one or more of his personal goals, he will tend to be a high producer. Conversely, if he sees low productivity as a path to the achievement of his goal, he will tend to be a low producer." [9] However, they postulated that there is this contingency: a productivity path will be followed if there are no restraining forces or barriers blocking his path, and if other more desirable paths to the goals for which the individual has a high need are not open to him in the situation.

The empirical findings testing the proposition presented above, in a study of the performance of six hundred and twenty one workers in a manufacturing organization, supported the hypotheses. They found that of those workers who perceived high productivity as an instrument to earn more money in the long run, 38 percent were high producers, compared to 21 percent of those who did not; of those who perceived low productivity as hurting, 30 percent were high producers, compared to 22 percent among those viewing low productivity as helping or irrelevant. They concluded "the findings indicate that if a worker sees high (or low) productivity as a path to the attainment of his personal goals, he will tend to be a high (or low) producer. This relationship is more pronounced among workers who have a high need with respect to a given goal and who are free from constraining forces than among workers lacking these conditions. When compared across tables, the results also show that functionally high productivity viewed by the person as instrumental to the attainment of a goal does not operate differently from low productivity when the latter is viewed as impeding goal attainment and vice versa. In both cases the path-goal perception variable seems to be a significant determinant of individual productivity." [10]

Even though Georgopoulos et al.'s research is considered a serious attempt, many questions remain unanswered after its publication. They did not explain how other organizational variables could affect the productivity; neither did they explain how the degree of need satisfaction observed in the worker was produced. They did not explain how organizational or individual variables could affect path-goal perception. They also concluded that development of more adequate measures was necessary.

Vroom's (1964) approach to instrumentality represents the first

9. Ibid., p. 346.
10. Ibid., p. 352.

attempt to use cognitively-oriented assumptions as the basis for a general theory of work motivation.[11] According to him "the choices made by a person among alternative courses of action are lawfully related to psychological events occurring contemporaneously with the behavior." [12]

Vroom's model is built around the concepts of valence, expectancy, and force. He defines motivation as the "force" impelling a person to perform a particular action as determined by the interaction of (a) the person's expectancy that his act will be followed by a particular outcome and (b) the valence of the (first-level) outcome. This concept of force is basically equivalent to motivation and is shown to be the algebraic sum of the product of valences multiplied by expectancies.[13]

By valence, Vroom means the strength of an individual's preference for a particular outcome. This valence is a function of the "valences" of all other outcomes (second-level) and the first-level outcomes' instrumentality for the attainment of these other outcomes. First-level outcomes are the direct result of behavior (e.g., performing at certain levels) to achieve valence through their instrumentality for the securing of second-level outcomes, such as pay, promotion, recognition, etc., which may have a valence by themselves or which may have a valence because they lead to still other outcomes.

The major variable besides valence in Vroom's model is expectancy. According to Vroom an expectancy is defined as a momentary belief concerning the likelihood that a particular action will be followed by a particular outcome. Expectancies may be described in terms of their strength. Maximal strength is indicated by subjective certainty that the act will be followed by the outcome, while minimal (or zero) strength is indicated by subjective certainty that the act will not be followed by the outcome.[14]

This model presented by Vroom has been the basis for most of the subsequent work in this area.[15] Heneman and Schwab reviewed nine field studies which were conducted in order to test the formulation of expectancy theory proposed by Vroom, later

11. Victor Vroom, *Work and Motivation*, New York, John Wiley and Son, Inc., 1964.

12. *Ibid.*, p. 14.

13. *Ibid.*, p. 18.

14. *Ibid.*, p. 17.

15. William G. Scott and Terence Mitchell, *Organization Theory: A Structural and Behavioral Analysis*, Illinois, Irwin-Dorsey Co., 1972, p. 81.

by Porter and Lawler.[16] (Porter and Lawler's theory is discussed later in this chapter.) For example, Goodman, Rose, and Furcon (1970) interviewed 66 employees of a government research organization to obtain indications of the three most valent second-level outcomes, the instrumentality of seven factors for attaining these outcomes, and the amount of job control (in order to infer expectancy). A measure of force was derived for each of the seven factors. Actual measures of success on four of these seven factors were obtained and correlated with the appropriate force measure. Significant correlations were obtained in each instance. Heneman and Schwab also reported the study conducted by Galbraith and Cummings (1967). According to them, Galbraith and Cummings obtained ratings of the valence of seven second-level outcomes, and the instrumentality of performance for their attainment, from 32 operators in a manufacturing organization. Ability was measured by length of time on the job, and performance was measured by daily output as a percentage of standards averaged over a one month interval. The independent variables were dichotomized, coded in dummy variable format (including interaction variables), and subjected to stepwise multiple regression analysis. No valence instrumentality, or ability variables entered into any of the regression equations significantly, and only 6 of 54 possible interaction variables entered into the equations significantly.[17]

Galbraith used the motivational model suggested by Vroom to combine a number of variables which were hypothesized as influencing performance.[18] The results were generally in support of the Vroom model in that the interactions between valence and instrumentality were the most significant variables. According to him this finding gives some support to the multiplicative hypothesis concerning motivation and ability.

It would seem that this motivational model presented by Vroom represents a great contribution to the analysis of the determinants of performance. However, it has been criticized by a few academicians in the field. Some of them have tried to overcome the limita-

---

16. Herbert Heneman and Donald Schwab, «Evaluation of Research on Expectancy Theory Predictions of Employee Performance,» *Psychological Bulletin*, 1973, 78, pp. 1-9.

17. *Ibid.*, p. 3.

18. Jay Robert Galbraith, *Motivational Determinants of Job Performance*. Unpublished doctoral dissertation, Indiana University, 1966.

19. John P. Campbell *et al.*, *Managerial Behavior, Performance, and Effectiveness*, New York, McGraw-Hill Book Co., 1970, p. 345.

tions that they pointed out by the addition of more variables to the model or by proposing significant changes. For example, one of the basic critiques usually raised against Vroom's model is that it lacks explicitness in defining and distinguishing between task goals, first-level outcomes, and second-level outcomes. "Task goals might be things such as quotas, time limits, standards, or the expression of loyalty in positive attitudes for the firm. First level outcomes refer to incentives such as salary, promotion, responsibility, etc., while second-level outcomes refer to more basic needs such as food, housing or freedom from anxiety.[20] According to Campbell *et al.*, another limitation of Vroom's model is the necessity for a more concrete specification of the task or performance goals toward which work behavior is directed.[21]

Graen used role concepts in order to help in defining differences between first-level and second-level outcomes. According to him his model differs from Vroom's original model in two major respects: "First, this model distinguishes clearly between work roles and role outcomes, whereas Vroom's model at best implies the natures of different kinds of outcomes..." Second, the emphasis of the extended model on historical as opposed to ahistorical elements allows for better developmental studies of the formulation of work personality and work motivation. This orientation toward understanding the developmental processes of work motivation is the major advantage of the extended model." [22]

Graen and Galbraith (both cited before), Evans, and Porter and Lawler, each using somewhat different instrumentality-expectancy models, obtained promising results which provide a more substantive approach to the path-goal model of work behavior.

All of these models are modifications of Vroom's model and are also based upon the theories presented earlier by Peak (1955),[23] Atkinson (1958),[24] and Tolman (1959),[25] among others. They may be considered as elaborated path-goal models of work behavior.

---

20.   William Scott and T. Mitchell, *op. cit.*, p. 84.

21.   Campbell, *et al.*, *op. cit.*, p. 45.

22.   George Graen, «Instrumentality Theory of Work Motivation: Some Experimental Results in Suggested Modifications,» *Journal of Applied Psychology*, 1969, *53*, pp. 1-15.

23.   H. Peak, «Attittude and Motivation,» in M. R. Jones (ed.). *Nebraska Symposium on Motivation*, Lincoln, University of Nebraska Press, 1955.

24.   J. W. Atkinson, *op. cit.*

25.   E. Tolman, «Principles of Purposive Behavior,» in S. Koch (ed.), *Psychology: A Study of Science*, vol. 12, New York, McGraw-Hill, 1959.

AN ELABORATED PATH-GOAL MODEL OF WORK BEHAVIOR

As discussed in the last section, Graen presented a model which attempts to extend Vroom's model. Using a simulation, he tested the proposed addition to Vroom's model. Subjects working in a simulated organization were assigned randomly to the following three treatments: (a) a condition where favorable feedback of high achievement was perceived to be contingent upon effective performance, (b) a condition where subjects received an outcome of money which was not contingent upon effective performance, and (c) a control condition where subjects received neither achievement feedback nor money.

From this experimental simulation Graen concluded that "this study demonstrated that the job incumbent model can predict job satisfaction and that the effective performer model can predict both job satisfaction and job performance under certain conditions. In addition, this study demonstrated the predicted consequences of certain job experiences on perceived instrumentalities." [26]

In fact Graen argues that an important boundary condition for instrumentality theory is that contingencies must be established in a concrete manner between effective job performance and attaining favorable role outcomes.[27]

One of the contributions of this study was to present a condition or a set of conditions necessary in order that the model would predict performance. In addition the study showed that the perception of instrumentality relationship was responsive to the actual contingencies of the job situation rather than independent of the job environment.

Another recent model of work motivation was presented by Evans.[28] Evans attempts to extend the understanding of leadership behavior by examining the impact of a leader's behavior in terms of initiation of structure and consideration on the subordinates' path-goal instrumentalities. According to him, data relevant to the theoretical scheme in two organizations (a public utility—the sample consisted of 311 workers; and a general hospital—88 nurses) supported the theory presented.

---

26. George Graen, op. cit., p. 18.
27. Ibid., p. 19.
28. Martin G. Evans, «The Effects of Supervisory Behavior on the Path-Goal Relationship,» Journal of Organizational Behavior and Human Performance, 1970, 5, pp. 277-298.

Evans proposed that the perception of path-goal instrumentalities related to the behavior and goal attainment of the subjects. According to him "the data that have been presented here provide support for two interrelated theories. First, at a quite general level, more evidence in favor of the path-goal theory of motivation was presented (i.e. path-goal instrumentalities relate both to behavior and goal attainment). Second, it was shown that supervisory behavior can relate to the path-goal instrumentality in predictable ways; that when it does, then it also relates to worker satisfaction, while when it does not its relationship with worker satisfaction is weak." [29]

Thus, Graen and Evans showed that the basic propositions of Vroom's model are replicable. Furthermore, Evan's main contribution is to show that the perception of instrumentality in the job to obtain a goal may be affected by many factors and that for future research it is important to try to develop strategies to take these into account.

In 1968 in their book *Managerial Attitudes and Performance,* Porter and Lawler presented a model which attempts to explain the complex relationship that exists between job attitudes and job performance.[30] This model, like Vroom's model, is considered an important contribution to the understanding of job performance and satisfaction. As Heneman and Schwab said, "These formulations (referring to Vroom's model and Porter and Lawler's model) have stimulated considerable thought and research." [31] This multi-variable model counters some of the simplistic traditional assumptions made about the positive relationship between satisfaction and performance, for example, that satisfaction causes performance.

Like Vroom's model, Porter and Lawler's model is based upon an expectancy theory of motivation. But, especially in more recent refinements, the model incorporates much more than is found in traditional expectancy theories (e.g., that perception of equity affects the degree of satisfaction experienced by the individual in the organization and that role perception combines with effort and ability to produce performance), with past learning still playing a vital role. (Contrary to Vroom's theory which is ahistorical, Porter and Lawler proposed that the perception of being rewarded

---

29. *Ibid.,* p. 296.
30. Lyman Porter and E. Lawler, *Managerial Attitudes and Performance,* Illinois, Richard D. Irwin Publishing Co., 1968.
31. Heneman and Schwab, *op. cit.,* p. 1.

affects the individual's perception of instrumentality in the future.)

The purpose of Porter and Lawler's model is to predict individual performance. According to them performance is the product of the combination of effort, ability, and role perception.

An important proposition of this model is that effort is distinctly different from performance. According to them the amount of effort depends upon the interaction between the value of the reward and the perceived effort-reward probability.

For Porter and Lawler, the value placed on a reward depends on its degree of attractivenes and desirability and that along with the perceived effort-reward probability is the other major input into effort. 'Effort-reward probability' refers to the employee's perception of the probability that differential rewards depend upon differential amounts of effort. In interactive combination, these two variables (value of reward and perception of effort-reward probability) determine the amount of effort that will be exerted. If an employee places a high value on a reward, and if he perceives a high probability that his effort will lead to this reward, he will exert a great deal of effort.

Performance represents the pragmatic result that organizations are able to measure objetively. Effort leads to performance, but the two cannot be automatically equated. A discrepancy between effort and performance may result from the employee's abilities and traits and/or his role perceptions.

Porter and Lawler's model included two kinds of reward: extrinsic and intrinsic. Both are desirable by definition. However, the intrinsic rewards are much more likely to produce attitudes of satisfaction that are related to performance. In addition, the perceived equitability of the rewards received vitally affect the reward satisfaction relationship. Equitability reflects the fair level of rewards that the individual feels should be granted for a given level of performance. Satisfaction with rewards is modified by the extent to which actual rewards fall short, meet, or exceed the person's perceived equitable level of rewards. Therefore, if actual rewards meet or exceed perceived equitable rewards, then the individual will be satisfied. Porter and Lawler's explanation of satisfaction makes two important departures from traditional thinking about satisfaction. First, the model recognizes that satisfaction is only in part determined by actual rewards received. It depends also on what a person feels the organization should reward for a given level of performance. Second, the model recognizes satisfaction to be more dependent on performance than performance is on satisfaction.

This model has been partially tested by Porter and Lawler and other academicians. Some of the results support Porter and Lawler's theory and others fail to support it. According to Heneman and Schwab the results obtained by Porter and Lawler offered some support for the their theory: "Porter and Lawler (1968) investigated the effect of valence of pay, instrumentality, and role perceptions on the performance of 635 managers. These variables were measured as in the Lawler and Porter (1967) study. Dependent measures were self-ratings and supervisory rankings of effort and performance. Hypotheses were tested by the significance of difference between mean performance and effort of managers giving the highest and lowest third of responses to the independent variable(s) in question. In general the results offered some support for the main effect of instrumentality and role perceptions. Less support was obtained for hypothesized interaction effect." [32]

Mitchell and Pollard testing this theory in an academic setting obtained support for it.[33] They used two measures of effort: the number of hours that the faculty spent in teaching, research, administrative work, and community service per week, and the professor's self-rating of the amount of effort exerted on the job. The correlation obtained between actual time spent and expectancy times instrumentality times valence was .27 ($p < .05$; $N = 50$) and .33 ($p < .01$; $N = 54$) when the self-effort rating was used.[34]

According to Mitchell and Pollard, the job performance results were mixed. The self-rating model (self-rating of ability, role perception, and effort) produce and r of .47 ($p < .01$) and an r of 48 ($p < .05$) with the dean rating; produced an r of .29 (non significant) and an r of .20 (non significant) with peer rating, and produced an r of .25 ($p < .05$) and a non significant r of .34 with the publications index. The peer ratings also produced significant and non-significant correlations with the three indexes of performance used.[35]

Pritchard and De Leo created a laboratory simulation in order to test the expectancy-valence models of work.[36] They set outcome valences at two levels, high and low, by establishing two different

32. Heneman and Schwab, op. cit., p. 3.
33. Terence Mitchell and W. Pollard, «Effort, Ability, and Role Perception as Predictor of Job Performance,» Washington, University of Washington, 1973.
34. Ibid., p. 6.
35. Ibid., p. 9.
36. Robert D. Pritchard and Phillip De Leo, «Experimental Test of the Valence-Instrumentality Relationship in Job Performance,» Journal of Applied Psychology, 1973, 51, pp. 264-270.

pay rates and they determined performance-outcome instrumentalities by paying hourly (low instrumentality) or by piece rate (high instrumentality). They found that while each variable affected performance they did not interactively affect performance. "While the analysis of variance indicated there was a main effect due to instrumentality ($F = 7.61$, df $= 56$, $p < .01$), the cell means show that this effect is due to subjects in the low-valence-high instrumentality condition strongly outperforming all other subjects. The high-valence-high-instrumentality subjects did not demonstrate higher performance than the low-instrumentality-high-valence subjects as had been predicted.[37]

Another study designed in order to test the expectancy theory was conducted by Jorgenson, Dunnette, and Pritchard.[38] In this study an experimental manipulation of a performance-reward contingency was carried out on a sample of 256 male college students who were hired to work six consecutive days under simulated work conditions, three days under a high performance-reward contingency condition and three days under low contingency condition. This manipulation was examined for its effects on the subjects' perceived effort-pay probability, perceived effort performance and valence of pay.

They reported that as predicted there was a significant difference between high and low expectancy conditions in perceived effort-pay probabilities. There was also a significant interaction between order and expectancy but there was no significant difference in the perceived amount of effort exerted under the two expectancy conditions.[39]

Lawler and Suttle concluded that the previous research done in order to test expectancy theory failed to consider a number of crucial aspects: "The studies designed to test expectancy theory have consistently found that the expectancy-type attitude measures are significantly correlated with measures of job performance. Nevertheless, a number of crucial aspects of the theory remain untested and a number of important questions remain unanswered." [40]

---

37. *Ibid.*, p. 267.

38. Dale O. Jorgenson, Marvin Dunnette, and Robert Pritchard, «Effects of the Manipulation of a Performance-Reward Contingency on Behavior in a Simulated Work Setting,» *Journal of Applied Psychology*, 1973, 57, pp. 271-280.

39. *Ibid.*, p. 276.

40. E. Lawler and J. Suttle, «Expectancy Theory and Job Behavior,» *Journal of Organization Behavior and Human Performance*, 1973, 9, 482-503, p. 503.

As they showed in their review, a majority of the studies have tried to test the relative validity of different forms of the expectancy model. That is, they have tried to determine such things as whether or not multiplying expectancy attitudes and valence attitudes leads to improved prediction of behavior. But they found that, unfortunately, few studies have measured all the different kinds of attitudes that are necessary for a complete test.

Hence many studies have measured how the perception that performance factors influence pay, given that pay is an attractive reward to the individual, affects the amount of effort exerted by the worker on the job. However, not many studies considered how other rewards may affect the individual's behavior. As Campbell *et al.*, have said, "A small amount of information is available concerning the expressed preferences of managers for various types of pay plans. In general, managers tend to prefer their compensation in straight salary rather than in various types of fringe benefits. However, this generalization is based on rather limited information, and there may be a substantial discontinuity in preferences as salary increases. At the lower salary levels there might be a greater preference for fringe benefits and other rewards instrumental in satisfying the need for security, while at higher levels, money could take on greater instrumentality for status and achievement of needs." [41]

Another area that has been missed in the previous research is the impact of organizational variables and situational variables on the individual's perception of instrumentality and on his expectations. Variables such as trust, warmth, participation in the decision making process, have not been considered as possible intervening variables of individual work perceptions. Furthermore, as Heneman and Schwab have concluded, "The effects of role perceptions has been investigated in few studies. However, no attempt was made to tap role perception accuracy as defined by Porter and Lawler." [42] According to these authors, more attention should be devoted to accuracy of role perceptions in future research. Additionally, it seems that more meaningful measures would concentrate on the inclusion of the job duties and objectives derived from detailed analysis of the specific job under consideration. It is these duties and requirements that ultimately define the individual's job and form the basis of his performance evaluation.[43]

41. Scott and Mitchell, op. cit., p. 84.
42. Heneman and Schwab, *op. cit.*, p. 6.
43. *Ibid.*, p. 7.

In general, while Porter and Lawler's elaborated model of the path-goal theory of work motivation has been studied in bits and pieces, three aspects of the model have not been given sufficient treatment. The *first* is the *feedback mechanism* implicit in the model; that is, the relationship between the rewards at t_2 resulting from performances at t_1 and the perceived effort-reward probability at t_3 and the relationship between rewards-satisfaction at t_2 and perceived equitable rewards at t_2 and the value of rewards at t_3.

The *second* is the position of *role* perceptions, and more broadly, the part role theory plays in the interaction of the model's variables.

The *third* is the salience of *organizational* attitudes (other than equity) in the performance of the model.

The first of these problems will not be treated here in as much as a time serial study was not feasible. The second and third problems will be studied in this research and are considered to be the major advances put forth by this dissertation.

THE FUNCTION OF ROLE PERCEPTION IN THE ELABORATED PATH-GOAL MODEL OF WORK BEHAVIOR

The model presented by Porter and Lawler indicates that the appropriateness of an individual's role perception has an important influence on his performance and the organization's rewarding of his performance. However, their model does not attempt to specify what the correct role perceptions are likely to be in a given situation. The model merely points out that if an individual's role perception is inappropriate for his job then good performance is unlikely.

According to Porter and Lawler's theory, role perception is one of the variables essential in determining performance. They hypothesized that performance is a function of the three-way interaction between exerted effort, ability, and role perception.

The function of the variable of role perception in the model is to determine if the effort exerted by the individual goes in the right direction. They said, "If his perception of his role (referring to individual role perception) corresponds to those of his superiors in his organization, then he will be applying his effort where it will count the most for successful performance as defined by the organization." [44] They tried to test this proposition by asking the

---

44. Porter and Lawler, *op. cit.*, p. 40.

manager to rank a number of psychological traits in order of perceived importance for determining success in their present position. We consider, as Stryker inferred,[45] that while the model
proposes the measurement of role perception accuracy (consensus
between subordinate and superior definition of role) "by defining
the traits with one word it is doubtful that even approximately
equal meanings are triggered for all respondents." (Quotation presented by Heneman and Schwab in their discussion of this topic).[46]
With Heneman and Schwab, we believe that more attention should
be devoted to accuracy of role perceptions.[47]

This study attempts to overcome this limitation through the
development of a new variable: the organization role expectation.
We define this variable as the perception of organizational administration about the kind of activities and behavior that they consider individuals should engage in to perform their job successfully.
Thus, through information about subordinates' definitions of their
roles and the superior's definition of the roles in which subordinates should engage in order to produce good performance, we
should be able to gauge the degree of accuracy of role perceptions.

So far few studies have measured the function of the role perception in the Porter and Lawler model. Porter and Lawler (1968),
using the method mentioned above, found that role perception can
have an influence on job performance. "Since the present study
is not of an experimental nature, it is impossible to determine with
certainty whether or not the relationship found between role
perceptions and performance came about as the model predicted,
role perceptions moderating the relationship between effort and
performance. Strictly speaking, all that our data proves is that
role perceptions and performance are related.[48]

However, since they did not determine the degree of accuracy
in role perceptions, they were not able to test the relationship
proposed in their model: performance is the function of the interaction of effort, ability and role perception.

According to the Porter and Lawler results, inner directed people
are more effective in performing their managerial job.[49] Going
upon these findings, Lawler and Suttle used the inner-other scale

45. P. Stryker, «On the Meaning of Executive Qualities,» Fortune, 1958,
57, pp. 116-119.
46. Heneman and Schwab, op. cit., p. 6.
47. Ibid., p. 7.
48. Porter and Lawler, Managerial Attitudes and Performance, op. cit.,
p. 114.
49. Ibid., p. 114.

to measure role perception and to test the model proposed by Porter and Lawler. According to their findings, role perception tends to be the best predictor of the performance rankings, but neither the additive combination nor the multiplicative one correlates very highly with performance. They concluded that "The results provide little support for the argument that a multiplicative combination of ability, role perceptions, and expectancy beliefs is the best predictor of job performance. The results do show that some combination of these factors can significantly predict performance." [50]

Lawler and Suttle used two measures of role perception: job behavior and job success (for an explanation of the way they designed this index see page 10 of their article already cited).

They claimed that although role performance was the best predictor of performance, neither the indexes of job behavior nor of job success produced higher coefficients. Job behavior produced a coefficient of .05 (non significant) with the self rating of performance, .24 ($p < .05$) with the superior's rating of performance, .15 (non significant) with the peers' rating, and −.05 with their objective measure of performance (sales produced by the subjects). Job success correlated −.01 with the boss measure of performance, .32 ($p < .01$) with the peers' rating, and −.34 ($p. < .01$) with the sales rating.

Mitchell and Pollard also tested the model proposed by Porter and Lawler's theory. However, they did not measure role perception as Porter and Lawler did. "Each subject rated himself and his role set member on how optimally they distribute their time among activities in such a way as to meet the expectation of their peers and the dean. The correlation was $r = .32$ ($p < .01$; $n = 55$).[51]

Like Lawler and Suttle they use the superior's rating of performance, in this case the dean's rating, the peer rating, and an objective measure of performance (the number of publications of each professor).

They concluded that their job performance model received fairly good support. All three predictor variables (ability, role perception, and effort) were related to performance although none of the combinations of these variables that were investigated was significantly better than any other.

The two measures of role perception produced the following

50. Lawler and Suttle, op. cit., p. 18.
51. Mitchell and Pollard, op. cit., p. 5.

2.

correlations with the index of performance. The self role perception produced a correlation of .11 (non significant) with the dean rating, .23 (non significant) with the peer rating, and .24 (p < .05 with the publications rating. The peer role perceptions produced a correlation coefficient of .18 (non significant) with the dean's rating, .35 (p < .01) with the peer rating, and .36 (p. < .01) with the publication rating.

As in the research of Lawler and Suttle the results of the correlation of the measures of role perception were mixed. They produced a significant correlation coefficient with some of the measures of performance and non significant correlation with the others.

As Heneman and Schwab, and Mitchell and Pollard, indicated, few studies so far have tested the function of the role perception variable in the Porter and Lawler model. Heneman and Schwab stated "the effects of role perception have also been investigated in only three instances." [52] Mitchell and Pollard concluded "Porter and Lawler (1968) and Galvin (1970) provide only weak support for these ideas and their investigations have been the only ones to date which have tested this more inclusive model." [53] Also the results obtained in these studies were not strong. Therefore, we believe that further research is necessary.

We believe that this research should include design measures of role perception that tap the role perception accuracy as defined by Porter and Lawler. It is our position that neither the Porter and Lawler research nor that of Lawler and Suttle, nor the Mitchell and Pollard study fulfilled this requirement. Porter and Lawler merely asked managers to rank a number of psychological traits in order or perceived importance for determining success in their present position. Lawler and Suttle assuming the Porter and Lawler conclusion used the inner-other scale to design two indexes of role perception; Mitchell and Pollard used self rating and peer rating measures on how optimally faculty distribute their time among activities in such a way as to meet the expectation of their peers and the dean. In all of these studies the subordinate's role perception and the superior's role expectation were compared to determine the degree of accuracy of the role perception. However, we feel that role content needs to be made more explicit in this procedure. We propose to improve the measurement of the role

---

52. Heneman and Schwab, *op. cit.*, p. 6.
53. Mitchell and Pollard, *op. cit.*, p. 3.

perception variable through the inclusion of the job duties and objectives derived from detailed analysis of the specific activities in which a professor would engage in his professorial position. Two indexes will be used in order to measure the degree of accuracy of role perception. One would include the typical activities in which a professor has to be involved at the university, such as research, teaching, and administrative duties. By asking the professor how he spends his time among these activities and by asking the chairman his opinion about how a professor should spend the time in his position, we hope to determine the degree of difference between the professor's role perception and the chairman's (his superior) role expectation and correlate these with performance evaluations. The second index would include a list of different activities which usually are considered to be included in the duties of a professor such as counseling students, work in committees, etc. Both the professor's and the chairman's opinions about the degree of importance of each of these activities in the accomplishment of the university's objectives will be measured. This index should provide us with additional information about the degree of consensus of the role perception between the subordinate and his superior.

Even though there are not many studies which directly test the function of role perception in the elaborated path-goal model of work behavior, there exist some studies done on role perception in connection with performance and satisfaction which are relevant for the classification of the problem that we are analyzing.

We think that the analysis of these studies is relevant because it should provide additional information about the interaction of the variable role perception with the rest of the variables of the path-goal model.

Even though Porter and Lawler proposed that the accuracy of role perception is fundamental in order to produce relevant performance, its function in the model should not be limited to its interaction with ability and effort. Its association with other variables should have an important effect in the whole model. For example there is a line of research which analyzed how the degree of accuracy of role perception is related with the degree of satisfaction experienced by the individual in the organization. The model of Porter and Lawler's proposes a loop between satisfaction and the value of reward. The model assumes that when people obtain a reward through their performance at t_1, this experience would affect the value of the reward at t_2. We propose that it is possible to explain the degree of satisfaction experienced by people, not only by their perception of being properly rewarded, but additionally because of the role consensus that produced that satisfaction.

We believe that there is much research about role perception that can be utilized to understand the relation of the variable role perception in the path-goal model and which would help to understand results that the path-goal studies cannot explain.

Greene and Organ have already measured the role accuracy score for each subject in the way we propose (summing the differences between the responses of the focal person about his perceptions of what his superiors expect of him and his superior's responses to the items on the work analysis form), finding a correlation with performance (.35 at the level of significance of .001) evaluated by the superior as to each of the activities along a seven-point scale ranging from low to high performance.[54]

Even though the main objetive of this research was not the testing of the relation between performance and role accuracy, we considered its finding a sufficient support for our proposition, since the method followed in order to measure the variables was quite similar to the method we propose in this study.

On the other hand, Tosi, measuring effectiveness as the profitability of an office (ratio of the net profits for an office to the total amount of capital investment in that office), and role conflict and role ambiguity as the "incompatibilities or incongruities involved in perception of performance of role requirements, found no significant relation when role conflict and role ambiguity were correlated with effectiveness. The correlation between role conflict and affectiveness was .03 (non significant); role ambiguity correlated at .007 (non significant) with effectiveness.[55]

Another study in which role ambiguity and role conflict were correlated with organizational effectiveness and other variables was conducted by House and Rizzo.[56] They used measures of organizational and leadership practices as predictors. The dependent variables were satisfaction, perceived effectiveness, anxiety, and propensity to leave. The variables role conflict and role ambiguity were treated as predictor, intervening, and dependent variables in the model. According to the authors, role measure hypotheses were

54. *Ibid.*, p. 97.

55. Henry Tosi, «Organization Stress as a Moderator of the Relationship Between Influence and Role Response,» *Academy of Management Journal,* 1971, *14,* pp. 47-58.

56. Rober House and John Rizzo, «Role Conflict and Ambiguity as Critical Variables in a Model of Organizational Behavior,» *Organizational Behavior and Human Performance,* 1972, 7, pp. 467-505.

generally supported, and role ambiguity was a better predictor and intervening variable than role conflict.

House and Rizzo concluded, "role ambiguity accounted for between 30 and 75 percent of the magnitude of the zero-order correlations. Concerning the correlation between supportive leader behavior and perceived organizational effectiveness, it can be seen that role conflict contributed more to these correlations than did role ambiguity, and the joint contribution of the two role dimensions accounts for between 33 and 66 percent of the magnitude of the zero order correlations. Thus the contribution of the role dimensions to these correlations appears to be both statistically and theoretically significant." [57]

So far we see that the measures of role perception have produced significant results as predictors of performance or organizational effectiveness in some of the research that has been conducted. Although the problem of the function of the accuracy of the roles, and its associated problem of the way performance is ranked, have been considered in just one of the studies reported, the fact that role ambiguity and role conflict affect the degree of organizational effectivenes constitutes a good indicator. All of these studies showed that when for any reason there is a disagreement between the role required or assigned to the subordinate and his perception of what the proper role should be, the result is a decrease in organizational effectiveness. The role theorist explains this decrease in the degree of organizational effectiveness as a result of the lack of coordination of the individual's activities when there is no role clarity, role accuracy, or consensus.

The path-goal theory and the role theory also present explanations of the degree of satisfaction experienced by the people in the organization. According to the Porter and Lawler model, when organizational rewards are determined by individual performance the degree of satisfaction experienced by him in the organization would be a function of the perception of being rewarded with the desired and equitable reward.

Specifically, if the rewards in a university are determined by the quality of the performance of the professor, the satisfaction experienced by him would be a product of his perception of the attained reward (promotion, tenure, prestige, etc.), given that the professor considers that this is an equitable reward.

The Greene and Organ finding concerning the relation between

---

57. *Ibid.*, p. 499.

role accuracy and satisfaction is consistent to some extent with
Porter and Lawler's proposition. They found that role accuracy
operates as a pre-condition for compliance. "The results further
indicated that compliance, in turn, is a direct cause of satisfaction,
and also an indirect cause of satisfaction through its direct effect
on performance evaluation." [58] In other words, compliance is directly related to satisfaction when controlling for performance.

If compliance were a measurement of behavior as the superior
would prescribe it, the result of the Greene and Organ research
is quite consistent with the Porter and Lawler theory. Porter and
Lawler's model states that satisfaction is a function of being
rewarded because the superior perceives that the subordinate did
what he (the superior) considers he should do. Therefore, this is
similar to the role theory which says that to behave as the superior
expects will lead the subordinate to experience satisfaction. The
path-goal theory states that being engaged in the activities that the
superior considers appropriate will lead the superior to rank
the subordinate as a higher performer and therefore he (the subordinate) is rewarded more. Assuming that the subordinate considers the reward equitable he will experience satisfaction. From
the explanation of Greene and Organ we can infer that the satisfaction experienced by the subordinate is the function of being
rewarded because he behaves and perceives his role to be as his
superior expects him to.

Of course, the Greene and Organ finding is not the only explanation of the relation of role accuracy and satisfaction in role
theory. For example, one of the classical studies that is cited very
often in the literature of role theory is the Kahn et al. research.
According to them there is a direct association between role ambiguity and role conflict with satisfaction in the organization.[59]

THE DETERMINANTS OF ROLE DISAGREEMENTS

The path-goal model of work behavior assumes that there should
be a role consensus between the subordinate and the superior in
order for the subordinate's performance to be ranked as effective
by the superior. As mentioned above, role perception seems to be
a critical variable in this model; therefore, we consider quite im-

---

58. Greene and Organ, op. cit., p. 102.
59. Robert Kahn et al., Organizational Stress: Studies in Role Conflict
and Ambiguity, New York, John Wiley & Son, Inc., 1964, pp. 71-94.

portant the determination of which factors affect the degree of accuracy of role perception in the organization.

Role theory proposes that role behavior is a function of the role expectations of other relevant individuals. To understand and describe the means by which organizations obtain such predictable and dependable behavior, a number of role-related concepts are used by the role theorist. Kahn *et al.*, among others, use the following concepts that would explain a role episode. They define role as the set of activities associated with a given position which are defined as potential types of behavior. The role set consists of the members of an organization with whom an individual is directly associated. Role behavior is the recurring actions of an individual occupying an organizational position. Role expectation is the prescriptions and proscriptions held by members of a role set. Kahn *et al.* refer to members of a role set as "role senders" and to their communicated expectations as the "sent role". Role conflict is defined as the simultaneous occurrence of two (or more) role sendings, such that compliance with one would make more difficult compliance with the other.

The organization requires control of the behavior of its members in order to obtain its objectives. As De Vries said, "if the organizations are to function effectively, it would seem necessary that they have control over the behavior of their employees." [60]

Role conflict is produced in the process in which the organization seeks to control the work behavior of its members. According to Kahn *et al.*, role ambiguity and role conflict seem to be products of the demand for successful conformity under conditions of ceaseless and accelerating change. They said that "much of role conflict can be thought of as a kind of inadequate role sending; lack of agreement or coordination among role senders produces a pattern of sent expectations which contains logical incompatibilities or which takes inadequate account of the needs and ability of the focal person (the person who received the order)." [61]

A classical example of a situation which produces role conflict is when the individual simultaneously receives two or more sets of pressures, of which compliance with one would make more difficult compliance with the other. For example a professor experiences role conflict when the administration of the university requires

---

60. David L. DeVries, «The Relationship of Role Expectations to Faculty Behavior,» Center for Social Organization of Schools, The John Hopkins University, Baltimore, Maryland, Technical Report, 1972, pp. 72-73.

61. Kahn *et al.*, *op. cit.*, p. 21.

that course X cover certain material that his students (as referent others) consider inadequate or above their capability to understand.

It seems that with the framework provided by the role theory we can attain some understanding of the sources of role disagreement in the organization. We already stated that Porter and Lawlers' theory proposes that for a subordinate to produce effective performance he should engage in the activities considered relevant by his superior. Using the role theory concepts the subordinate must comply with his superior's expectations.

Which factors contribute to induce the subordinate into noncompliance with the role behavior expected by his supervisor? In addition to the factors mentioned by Kahn *et al.*, an endless number of factors may contribute to the disagreement between subordinate role behavior and superior role expectation. For example role behavior may be a function of attitudes or a predisposition to behave in a certain way.

However if the theory is to improve its explanatory power it must explain as much as possible of the individual's behavior in order to predict it. Therefore an attempt to provide some understanding of why the subordinate disagrees with his superior improves the explanatory power of the path-goal theory.

We propose that one of the predictors of the degree of agreement or disagreement between the subordinate and the superior is the degree of influence that relevant individuals may have upon subordinate behavior at the work setting. Therefore we consider that if we tap the individuals that may have influence upon subordinate behavior and determine the degree of influence that they can exert over him, we can predict if the superior will obtain compliance from his subordinate.

Since the subjects of this study are university professors we can use the research done about the sources of influence of academic professionals.

According to DeVries the literature on academic professionals suggests strongly that control over faculty is exercised primarily through interpersonal influence. He said that "given that control over academicians appears to operate largely through values shared by the professional community, role theory is a particularly appropriate framework for describing such control." [62]

Berlew and Hall's findings provide support for DeVries's con-

---

62. DeVries, *op. cit.*, p. 1.

clusion. They found that one of the strongest determinants of behavior is the expectations of other people.[63] In the language of the role theory, the behavior of a focal person is strongly influenced by the expectations of significant others, referred to as role senders.

According to DeVries an individual, in performing his various roles, is highly attuned to the actual and/or perceived reactions of a subset of other individuals in his environment.[64]

Therefore the degree of role agreement or disagreement between the profesors and the chairman would be determined by the amount of influence that he (the chairman) exerts upon the professors' behavior relative to the degree of influence that other role senders in the work setting may exert upon the professors' work behavior.

Determination of the role senders of the professors is necessary. It seems logical that a professor receives role messages from many role senders in the academic work setting. Using the Kahn *et al.* framework, we have to include in the group of role senders all the people with whom a professor works closely or has indirect relations. These include the chairman, departmental colleagues, the students who are taking courses from him, the general body of students, the dean of the school, colleagues in other universities and people outside of the university (even though the latter may be considered external to the environment of the university, we cannot forget that the professor fulfills expectations in which these people are relevant. Examples would be the president of a company in which he can get a consulting position or a politician that can appoint him to an important position in the government.)

All of these people or groups of people affect the behavior of a professor. If the chairman is not the source of the strongest influence upon the professor's behavior the result would be a role disagreement between the professor and the chairman. The degree of role accuracy should therefore be less.

Two theories seem useful for hypothesizing which of the sources of influence have greater influence upon the professor's behavior: the theory of Stinchcombe about the structure of attention and Raven's theory about social influence and power.

According to Stinchcombe the effect of someone else's activity on the actions and attitudes of a person is a function of the prob-

63. D. Berlew and D. T. Hall, «The Socialization of Managers: Effects of Expectation on Performance,» *Administrative Science Quarterly*, 1966, 2, pp. 207-223.

64. DeVries, *op. cit.*, p. 3.

ability that this person will pay attention to it, multiplied by the duration that the person's attention is focused on it.[65]

Therefore, the professor's role perception must be influenced by his perception of the expectation of each one of the people in his environment whom he considers relevant and who interacts with him very often. The greater the importance the professor ascribes to their opinion and the more frequently he interacts with them, the greater their influence upon his behavior.

However, we also must take into consideration that the relevance that a professor ascribes to each one of the sources of influence in his environment may vary according to their power.

According to Raven,[66] a person may influence the behavior of others through many kinds of power. Among others, coercive power, reward power, and expert power are sources of socially dependent influence. Raven considered that coercive power stems from the ability of the agent to mediate punishment for the influence. He said that reward power results from the ability of the agent to mediate rewards, and expert power stems from the attribution of superior knowledge or ability to the influencing agent.

We hypothesize that among all the persons who may influence the behavior of the professor those with more coercive, reward and expert power are going to be the persons with strongest influence.

Caplow and McGee,[67] argue that the departmental chairman, among all the people who form the environment of the professors, is the person who most likely has a unique combination of coercive, reward, and expert power to bring to bear on his influence attempts.

The chairman's evaluation is fundamental in the decision as to whether the professor deserves a reward or tenure, and the chairman decides the assignment of courses and the professor's schedule among other things. If the chairman has enough knowledge and ability he has expert power also. In other words he might have the three sources of power mentioned above.

Since the professor may also interact quite often with the chairman because they work together, we therefore believe that

65. Arthur L. Stinchcombe, *Constructing Social Theories*, Chicago, Harcourt, Brace and World, Inc., 1968, p. 236.

66. Bertram H. Raven, «Social Influence and Power,» Reading in I. D. Steiner and M. Fishbein (eds.), *Current Studies in Social Psychology*, New York, Holt, Reinhart, and Winston, 1965, pp. 371-382.

67. T. Caplow and R. J. McGee, *The Academic Marketplace*, New York, Basic Books, 1958.

the chairman is one of the persons with the strongest ability to influence the behavior of the professors in the university.

Kelman's (1958) psychologically based analysis of influence processes cited by Greene and Organ in their study offers support to my proposition. "The subordinate conforms to this superior's expectations not because he believes in their content, nor that conformity in itself is rewarding; but because he expects to gain approval or avoid a specific punishment." [68]

As a matter of fact Kelman's analysis offers support for the basic proposition of the path-goal theory. If the professor ascribes to the chairman the power to determine the rewards that he will obtain in the university, he may try to comply with the chairman's expectation. Therefore the degree of role accuracy between the professor and the chairman is a function of the professor's perception that the chairman is the person in his environment with most power to affect the rewarding process.

THE EFFECT OF THE ORGANIZATIONAL SETTING UPON THE PATH-GOAL MODEL OF WORK BEHAVIOR

One of the critiques usually stated against the path-goal model of work behavior is that it fails to provide a systematic and useful linkage between motivational and organizational variables.

The path-goal theorists followed the common tendency of social scientists to dichotomize the analysis of the organization into "studying organizations without people" or "studying people without organizations." The tendency of the social scientists has been to see human behavior in two different contexts, individual characteristics and properties of the social situation.[69]

Recently, some social scientists postulated the necessity of the integration of both approaches. For example, Lichtman and Hunt concluded "that the extreme variability found within and among organizations renders the one-sided normative theories less useful in understanding organizational behavior than models that recognize situational contingencies." [70]

McCarrey and Edwards hypothesized that the simultaneous in-

---

68. Greene and Organ, *op. cit.*, p. 101.
69. A good review of this problem or tendency in the social sciences was provided by Cary Lichtman and Raymond Hunt in their article «Personality and Organization Theory: A Review of Some Conceptual Literature,» *Psychological Bulletin*, 1971, 76, pp. 271-294.
70. Lichtman and Hunt, *op. cit.*, p. 271.

vestigation of the structuralistic orientation of the administrative theorists and the personalities orientation of the industrial psychologists would offer optimal return toward the understanding of organizational and human accomplishment. As a matter of fact, in their research they found that organizational climate, as perceived by role incumbents, and role performance, as assessed, were related.[71]

Inkson et al.'s proposition follows the same line of thought. They propose that "a more accurate understanding of the behavior of individuals and groups in organization is surely attendant upon a more accurate description of the context in which the behavior occurs, that is, the organization environment.[72] However, there have not as yet been many attempts in the social sciences to follow this approach and many fields of social science have been under recent criticism for this reason.

Some social psychologists have raised critiques against the path-goal models because they failed to consider the situational variables. For example Litwin and Stringer commented that "Vroom's theory, like many psychological theories, acknowledges the importance of situational variables, but does not provide a format by which such variables can be measured and mapped. Nor is there any way of relating the situational variables to sociological and organizational concepts of the situation." [73]

Like Litwin and Stringer, Schein states that there is a need for the establishment of links between motivational and organizational concepts. "It has been easy to accept organizational circumstances as a function of different motives... however, we cannot understand the psychological dynamic if we look only to the individual's motivations and practices. The two interact in a complex fashion requiring us to develop theories and research approaches which can deal with systems and interdependent phenomena." [74]

In their model Porter and Lawler do not take into account the environment of the organization as a general environment of the individual's path-goal activities. They state that "we should

71. Michael McCarrey and Shirley Edwards, «Organizational Climate Conditions for Effective Research Scientist Role Performance,» *Organizational Behavior and Human Performance*, 1973, 9, pp. 439-459.

72. J. H. Inkson et al., «Extending the Occupational Environment,» *Journal of Occupational Psychology*, 1972, *41*, 33-47, pp. 45-46.

73. G. Litwin and R. Stringer, *Motivation and Organizational Climate*, Boston, Harvard University, Graduate School of Business Administration, 1968, p. 31.

74. E. H. Schein, *Organizational Psychology*, Englewood Cliffs, Prentice Hall, 1965, pp. 64-65.

hasten to acknowledge that there are, obviously, many environmental factors that also intervene to influence the relationships
of effort to performance... In any case, our model does not take
into account such external environmental factors because they represent spurious factors in understanding the psychological and
human determinants of performance." [75]

We disagree with the position taken by Porter and Lawler. We
consider a model to be more useful when it can explain and
predict more degrees of variability in human behavior. If the social
setting of the organization has the relevance ascribed to it by the
social scientist cited before, it would be useful to consider its
effect upon the expectancy theory model (used here as synony-
mous with path-goal theory). Furthermore, Porter and Lawler's
inclusion of equity in their path-goal model already introduces the
specific organizational circumstance into their model as does the
rewarding process and organizational assessments of performance.
What is needed is a more thorough attempt at testing relevant
organizational conditions as these influence path-goal behavior.

In order to accomplish this objective it is fundamental to have
the definition of the variables in the social setting that we have to
consider as modifiers or intervening variables of the path-goal
model.

Some sets of criteria are necessary in order to determine which
are the relevant variables. Of course, the basic question we are
interested in is which variables would affect the degree of expectation or instrumentality that an individual perceives in the organization.

A useful criteria would be to select those variables that have
been associated with the dependent variables of the path-goal
model: effort, performance, and satisfaction.

If for example some studies conducted already have shown that
the feeling of red tape affects the degree of satisfaction experienced
by the individual in the organization, it would be useful to determine if this variable (red tape) is related to some extent with the
variables in Porter and Lawler's model. In addition special care
was taken in order to include in the literature review a significant
number of theoretical and empirical studies in the academic setting. The product of this analysis was a definition of the organizational setting with some structural and environmental variables.
All of these variables are demonstrated in theoretical and empirical
studies to be associated with the variables of the path-goal model.

---

75. Porter and Lawler, *op. cit.*, p. 43.

The following variables were consistent with the criteria stated before: academic freedom, perception of organizational warmth, participation in decision making, degree of structure of the organizational decision processes, trust, red tape, identification, and outsider power or influence in the organizational decision making process.

A study that supports the proposition that the structural and environmental variables affect the behavior of the individual in the organization and the predictive power of the path-goal model is Duncan's research. He found an association between the organizational environment and the attitudes and behavior of the individual in the organization. Duncan concluded that the "individual in decision units experiencing dynamic-complex environments experienced the greatest amount of uncertainty in decision making. The data also indicated that the static-dynamic dimension of the environment was a more important contribution to uncertainty than the simple-complex dimension." [76]

We consider Duncan's finding to be strong support for our proposition, because the expectancy model is based upon the perception of the individual that an attractive outcome may be obtained through his effort and performance. If the organizational environment may lead to uncertainty, the individual perception of the instrumentality of his performance can be affected. In other words the expectancy model would be affected by organizational environments.

Litwin and Stringer in a research conducted in two sales organizations concluded that the organizational climate is associated with individual motivation. They reported that "these data support quite strongly the initial theoretical assumption that the organizational climate is associated with individual motivation. They reported that "these data support quite strongly the initial theoretical assumption that the organizational climate concept would serve as a link between organizational and individual motivation variables." [77]

The findings of studies such as those reported already and the theoretical proposition of many researchers in the field provide us with some support for the proposition that the organizational setting may affect the path-goal model.

The decision to include some of the variables in the organiza-

---

76. Robert Duncan, «Characteristics of Organizational Environments and Perceived Environmental Uncertainty,» *Administrative Science Quarterly*, 1972, *17*, pp. 313-327.

77. Litwin and Stringer, *op. cit.*, p. 92.

tional setting was guided by some theoretical propositions presented in the field of higher education.

After a consideration of the theories that we are going to present in this section we concluded that an important variable in the environment of any university is the professor's perception of academic freedom.

It seems that the power of the academicians to determine their own goals, programs, and methods of evaluation is considered an inalienable right by the professors.

Many academicians (e.g., Nisbet) [78] have pointed to the necessity to defend academic freedom in America. Nisbet's essay is essentially concerned with the purpose of the academic community, which he sees to have been not only lost but violated, more or less deliberately if not systematically.

Professor Smith in one of the latest publications about academic freedom and tenure said, "Beyond the necessity of maintaining a climate of independence within higher education is the task of regaining a degree of independence from new forms of outside pressures." [79]

Another fact that shows how relevant academic freedom is for professors in the university is that the American Association of University Professors has been quite concerned with the freedom of the professors for self-determination in the universities.

All of these positions presented are useful to demonstrate how important the perception of academic freedom could be in shaping the behavior of the professors in the university.

It seems that many of the sources of satisfaction of their human needs are vested in the perception of academic freedom, since this power of the university to define its own tasks and responsibilities produces a sense of self-sufficiency and self-determination which fosters the perception of prestige, self-esteem, and self-actualization of the professors.

If the Hangstrom [80] hypothesis—that scientists are not motivated by the same kinds of extrinsic rewards as everybody else, namely position and money—is correct, the role of academic freedom is quite important in order to predict the behavior of the professors in the university. It can be seen as providing the professors with the sources to satisfy some of the intrinsic needs in their job.

78. R. Nisbet, *The Degradation of the Academic Dogma: The University in America, 1945-70*, New York, Basic Books, 1971.

79. B. L. Smith, *The Tenure Debate*, San Francisco, Jossey Bass, Inc., 1973, p. 222.

80. W. Hangstrom, *The Scientific Community*, New York, Basis Books, 1965.

In conclusion, it seems that the perception of academic freedom is considered a fundamental characteristic of the job of a professor in the university. Therefore, if we want to map the factors in the organizational environment that would affect the behavior of the professor we have to take into account the perception of academic freedom. Therefore we decided to include academic freedom in the organizational setting variables.

The decision to include the variable which attempts to measure the degree of influence or power of people outside of the university upon its relevant decisions was based upon a study conducted by the author in one of the regional colleges of the University of Puerto Rico. I found that one of the factors that professors mentioned as a source of dissatisfaction was the perception that people outside of the university have much power in the decision about the appointment of the chancellor of the university and other similar decisions. As a matter of fact all the research conducted in the field which shows that the environment produces uncertainty in the organizational members could be useful to predict the effect of the perception of the outsider power upon the behavior of the professor. As with any other dimension of the organizational climate this perception would produce uncertainty and would affect the degree of instrumentality that the professors perceive in the university.

Another variable included in the organizational setting is the degree of structure of the decision process. This variable is closely related to other variables included in the organizational setting. However, it attempts to measure how the fact that there are some guidelines in the decision making process affects the degree of uncertainty and of course the perception of instrumentality of the individual in the organization. Like the variable which attempts to tap the perception of the professors about the power of people outside of the university to influence the university decision making process, this variable is related to all the research reported here which states that the degree of uncertainty produced by the organizational environment would produce attitudes in the individual that would affect the path-goal model.

Researchers have found that a climate of warmth is relevant to the production of satisfaction and identification with the organization. Litwin and Stringer concluded "that it is reasonable to assume that such basic affiliative concern is critical in understanding others and in building good working relationships with both superiors and subordinates—this affiliative concern is a means to attain other, broader kinds of satisfaction, and might well be labeled interpersonal competence." [81]

They found that "warmth climates" appear to be appropriate in areas where the work requires building close relationships. It might also be appropriate in situations where highly competent and motivated people are working on very specialized tasks and where some non-coercive means for generating organizational cohesion and team spirit seems required. Generally, some degree of affiliation-orientation would seem to be appropriate in large, complex organizations where close coordination and integration of different functions is required. They also concluded that in education and therapeutic settings "warmth climates" might be used to encourage the establishment of closer, more feeling-oriented relationships and to facilitate the development of interpersonal sensitivity and skill.

Like Litwin and Stringer, other theorists have considered the "warmth climate" important in order to develop attitudes in organizational members which may affect their performance and satisfaction in the organization. McGregor (1960) views employee-centered warmth and support as a necessary condition in "theory Y" management.[82] Vroom's concept called "consideration" is somewhat parallel with our concept of warmth of climate. According to him, consideration includes supervisory behavior indicative of friendship, mutual trust, respect, and warmth. "There is considerable evidence that the satisfaction of subordinates is related to the consideration or employee orientation of their superior. In a study of 29 aircraft commanders, Halpin and Winer (1957) found a correlation of .64 between consideration as measured by the Leader Behavior Description Questionnaire and an index of crew satisfaction. A later investigation by Halpin (1957) reported a positive relationship between the consideration of school superintendents and the job satisfaction of elementary school teachers; Fleishman, Harris, and Burtt (1955) have found a positive relationship between the consideration of foremen and the morale of their subordinates." [83]

Likert (1961) recognized the relevance of a supportive atmosphere in the development of positive attitudes toward the organization. He said "there should be favorable, cooperative attitudes,

---

81. Litwin and Stringer, *op. cit.*, p. 23.
82. Douglas McGregor, *The Human Side of Enterprise*, New York, McGraw-Hill Book Co., 1960.
83. Victor Vroom, *op. cit.*, p. 110.

throughout the organization, with mutual trust and confidence." [84]

In synthesis warmth climates seem appropriate in order to develop good interpersonal relationships that are fundamental for satisfaction to be present in the organization.

This variable would seem to be relevant in predicting the degree of satisfaction that the individual experiences in the organization, satisfaction being one of the outcomes of the expectancy model.

Another variable evident in the organizational setting is red tape. "Red tape" usually is defined as the feeling that excessive rules, administrative details, etc., make it difficult for the employee to do his job in an adequate way.

We consider this variable to be closely related with the perception of academic freedom experienced by a professor at the university. Professors want to have a higher degree of independence in their job. Usually perception of red tape produces a lot of friction between professors and the administration of the university because the professors find too often that administrators require many procedures and regulations which to some extent impede professorial activities.

Eble, in his analysis of how the teaching environment should motivate or enable faculty members to function as good teachers, reports that Jerry Gaff and Robert Wilson, psychologists at the Center for Research and Development in Higher Education of the University of California at Berkeley found that the red tape which has to be cut through in any attempt to move teaching out of its ordinary routines—among others—adversely affects a teacher's perception of how well teaching is supported.[85]

Eckert and Stechlein,[86] in their study of job motivation and satisfaction of college teachers, found that dissatisfaction with aspects of college teaching careers focused on poor relations with colleagues, administrative red tape, and inadequate facilities. The Eckert and Anderson study in 1968,[87] showed similar results. Both college and university professors complain about administrative red tape.

84. R. Likert, *New Patterns of Management*, New York, McGraw-Hill Book Co., 1961.

85. Kenneth E. Eble, *Professors as Teachers*, California, Jossey Bass, Inc., 1972. p. 145.

86. R. E. Eckert and J. E. Stecklein, *Job Motivations and Satisfactions of College Teachers*, Cooperative Research Monograph, No. 7, U. S. Government Printing Office, 1961.

87. R. E. Eckert and D. Anderson, *The University of Minnesota Faculty: Who Serves and Why?*, Minneapolis, University of Minnesota, 1970.

We decided to include this variable in the organizational setting because it seems that one of the main effects of the perception of red tape in the university is to decrease the professor's perception that his effort will lead to a preferred performance and therefore to the attainment of intrinsic job satisfactions. Hence, we think that this variable would be relevant in the analysis of how the organizational setting can affect individual expectations in the organization.

Another organizational variable that we believe affects the individual's expectation and sense of instrumentality in the organization is his degree of trust in it. According to Zand, trust is defined as the individual's actions that increase his vulnerability to others whose behavior one cannot control.[88]

As with many of the environmental and organizational variables discussed already, trust is a powerful variable that affects individual expectation and perception of instrumentality in the organization. Like the climate of warmth, the trust climate is fundamental in order to facilitate interpersonal acceptance and openness of expression. There is increasing research evidence that trust is a salient factor in determining the effectiveness of many relationships.[89] For example, Gibb found that mistrust evokes interpersonal rejection and arouses defensive behavior.[90]

The importance of this variable increases when we are dealing with professors at universities. The kind of job these scientists and humanists have requires good interpersonal relation in order to get optimum effectiveness. We consider the communication of the professors fundamental in order to discuss innovations and project findings. In the area of publications and innovations much effort is required of many academicians: critiques, new approaches to problems, redefinitions of situations, etc. The motivation to work voluminously requires a great deal of co-worker participation. Human beings need to show their achievements and the best audience is the co-workers in the organization.

The presence, or lack, of trust might affect the possibilities that the individual will obtain satisfaction in his position. The degree of trust that the individual perceives in the organization might affect his expectation and is a fundamental feed-back rein-

---

88. D. E. Zand, «Trust and Managerial Problem Solving,» *Administrative Science Quarterly*, 1972, *17*, pp. 229-239.

89. J. R. Gibb, «Defensive Communication,» Reading in D. Kolb *et al.*, *Organizational Psychology*, New Jersey, Prentice Hall, 1974.

90. *Ibid.*, p. 237.

forcing his behavior. If a professor sees that, after he has accepted a position in a university, the administration does not keep its promises, he is not going to remain very committed to the organization. If he sees, for instance, that his coworker after five years of doing an excellent job did not get tenure he is not going to trust this organization.

In synthesis, trust is fundamental in order for individuals to maintain their expectations and is relevant for the existence of adequate interpersonal relations and therefore an organizational climate that develops satisfaction and increases the degree of involvement of the individual at the organization.

Therefore, we believe that the lack of trust in the organization would affect individual performance, satisfaction and identification, among other factors.

Another source of dissatisfaction that the professors mentioned in the survey we conducted in one of the regional colleges of the University of Puerto Rico was the lack of participation in the relevant decision making process. (This research was conducted in 1973 by the author.) This variable was shown to be related in many studies to the individual's attitudes toward the organization.

According to Alutto and Belasco in reviewing the literature on individual participation, at least three distinct themes emerge: (1) the first concerns the importance of decisional participation by employees in determining the acceptance of organizational change; (2) the second major area of research concentrates on interactions between the decisional participation rates of subordinates and the perceived relative influence of administrative superiors; and (3) the third focuses on the more generalized positive effects of employee participation in decision making.[91]

We consider that the third area of research should provide meaningful information concerning the problem that we are analyzing. We are interested in seeing what attitudes would be developed when the individual in the organization is allowed to participate in the relevant decision making process. If these attitudes affect to some extent the expectancy model, we can include the variable participation in the decision making process in the organizational setting.

A relevant study was conducted by Patchen in 1970. He analyzed the relationship between decisional participation and job satis-

---

91. Joseph Alutto and James Belasco, «A Typology for Participation in Organizational Decision Making,» *Administrative Science Quarterly*, 1972, *17*, pp. 117-125.

faction on one hand and job achievement and organizational integration on the other.[92] His research among TVA employees suggests that increased participation in institutional decision making leads to greater job satisfaction and work achievement as well as greater individual integration into the organization. It would seem that participation in the decisional process should permit the employees to not only increase their perception of instrumentality on the job but also it should affect role perceptions (via organizational integration) and job satisfaction.

Another study which showed that participation in the decisional process would have substantial impact upon the employee attitudes, beliefs, and motivation was that of Siegel and Ruh. Siegel and Ruh found that participation in decision making correlated with the degree of job involvement in the organization. They found a coefficient of .51 at .001 level of significance.[93]

Juralewicz conducted a study in Puerto Rico trying to test the hypothesis that there is a relationship between participation and the individual's performance and his job attitudes. He hypothesized that a high degree of participation by workers in decisions affecting their work strengthens their motivation to carry out these decisions. He found that the group that experienced moderate participation in the decisional process had the higher production level. The study did not show significant correlation between participation and attitudes toward work.[94]

Juralewicz concluded that the explanation of the lack of significant association between participation and attitude toward the job was that "not all employees center their lives in their jobs. Some employees find little satisfaction in their work so the opportunities offered to participate in decision-making are accepted with apathy and indifference. Their lives are centered in the home and the community so that they do not feel imposed on by the autocratic leadership style of management." [95]

Even though these findings did not support the typical hypothesis that participation affects the attitude of the employees at

92. Martin Patchen, *Participation, Achievement, and Involvement on the Job*, Englewood Cliffs, Prentice Hall, 1970.

93. Alan Siegel and Robert Ruh, «Job Involvement, Participation in Decision Making, Personal Background, and Job Behavior,» *Organizational Behavior and Human Performance*, 1973, 9, pp. 318-327.

94. R. S. Juralewicz, «Interpersonal Dimensions of Decision Making in a Cross-Cultural Setting,» Graduate School of Business, University of Puerto Rico, 1972.

95. *Ibid.*, p. 23.

work it did show a significant correlation with individual performance.

The fact that this study was conducted in Puerto Rico and did not support the generally accepted hypothesis that participation is related to attitude toward the work is another reason to include the participation variable in our study. Although the type of subject is different (Juralewicz's study was conducted with lower level workers in a company) we can see if culture will affect the relationship between participation in the decisional processes and the work performances and attitudes of the individuals in the organization.

According to Kavcic, Rus and Tannenbaum, the studies included in their research of the literature (Adizes, 1968; De Leon, 1956; Dunlop, 1959; Kolaja, 1965; Kraij, 1969; Mandie, 1958; and Sturn-mthal, 1964) showed that participation in the decisional process in the organization improves communication, increases confidence and trust among members, increases their involvement, improves their motivation, and maintains their support for the organization and its objectives.[96]

Even though some studies have produced non-significant results it seems that the participation in the decisional process has some effect upon the behavior of the individual in the organization. We considered that this attitude would affect the path-goal model to some extent and therefore it was included in the organizational setting of our research.

The last variable included in the organizational setting was identification. Litwin and Stringer in their justifications for using "identity" as a dimension of organizational climate said: "Berkowitz and Levy (1956), Berkowitz, Levy, and Harvey (1957), Pryer and Bass (1959), Hall (1957), and Zander and Wolfe (1964) have all studied the effects of different kinds of feedback patterns on individual performance, interpersonal orientations (such as feelings of trust, openness), worker satisfaction, and group cohesiveness. It was found that emphasizing group loyalty and group goals (i.e. only providing feedback of how the group was doing) increased group identity, and led to improved performance, less concern about personal rewards, more mutual trust, and less strain in interpersonal relations. Deemphasizing group goals (giving only individual feedback) led to more withdrawal from interpersonal

---

96. Bogdan Kavcic, et al., «Control, Participation, and Effectiveness in Four Yugoslav Industrial Organizations,» Administrative Science Quarterly, 1971, 16, pp. 74-87.

interaction, less desire to achieve a good score, and less mutual trust. When both personal and group goals were emphasized (when there was a feedback of how the group was doing and how individuals were doing), there was the greatest increase in personal performance, interpersonal sensitivity was increased, and task organization (division of labor) was most prevalent (see Zander and Wolfe, 1964, pp. 67-68). These results reflect some of the different motivational effects that group identity and loyalty may have on organizational behavior.[97]

The relevance of this research reported by Litwin and Stringer is not only that the degree of identification may affect organizational behavior, but also that the types of attitudes induced by the feeling of identification (trust, interpersonal interaction) are considered to be quite important if they are associated with the variables in the path-goal model. As we stated above, the relevance of the variables in the organizational setting would be that they affect the degree of instrumentality perceived by the individual in the organization. If identification produced trust, for example, it would affect the expectancy model because in order for an individual to exert effort in a situation he must trust that at the end his performance will be rewarded.

According to Gouldner (1954)[98] and Etzioni (1964)[99] among others, there is a basic incompatibility between professionals and organization. If the professors in the universities behave as these theories propose, all the findings reported above about the attitudes developed by the organizational members when they have the feeling of identification are irrelevant.

Bennis et al.,[100] and Glaser[101] have concluded that it has only infrequently been recognized that organizational professionals may be committed both to their profession and their organizations.

However, Thornton's findings about organizational involvement and commitment to both organization and profession represent a promising result. Thornton found that professional and organizational commitments can be compatible under certain conditions.

97. Litwin and Stringer, op. cit., p. 60.
98. Alvin Gouldner, Patterns of Industrial Bureaucracy, Glencoe: Free Press, 1954.
99. Amitai Etzioni, Modern Organizations, Englewood Cliffs, Prentice Hall, 1964.
100. W. G. Bennis et al., «The Nature of Profession,» in Nelson B. Henry (ed.), Education for the Professions 27-42, Chicago, University of Chicago, 1962.
101. Barney Glaser, «The Local-Cosmopolitan Scientist,» American Journal of Sociology, 1963, 69, pp. 249-259.

Generally, the extent to which the organizational professional experiences and perceives an organizational situation as reaffirming and exemplifying certain principles of professionalism determines the compatibility of the two commitments." [102]

The fact that Thornton's research was conducted among professors of junior colleges make the findings more appropriate to our discussion because our subjects are also professors. Also, Hall and Lawler found that the professional would be integrated within the organization given certain conditions in the job.[103] These findings encourage us to include identity as a variable which may well affect the professors efforts, performances and satisfaction.

The reason we decided to see the effect of the organizational setting upon the path-goal model is that we considered that these variables would affect to some extent the outcome of the model.

We hypothesized that the organizational variables would affect the expectancy model in different ways. For example, a variable in the organizational setting would affect the degree of instrumentality that the individual perceived in the organization. The presence of one of the variables included in the organizational setting may affect the relationship between two variables in the path-goal model. In addition, there is the possibility that the organizational setting explains more variability in the dependent variables than the combination of variables that the expectancy theory proposes to produce performance, effort, or satisfaction.

The model proposed by Porter and Lawler states that when the individual sees that the organization would provide him with a desired reward, and he perceives that his effort is instrumental in getting this reward, he would exert more effort.

We hypothesize that the organizational setting would affect this combination of variables that lead to effort.

For example, we defined structure as the professor's perception that there are guidelines in the decisional process of the relevant decisions, such as determination if the professor deserves tenure, promotion, and many other rewards.

If the professor considers that the obtaining of tenure in the university is important for him, his perception that this reward

102. Russell Thornton, «Organizational, Involvement and Commitment to Organization and Profession,» *Administrative Science Quarterly*, 1970, *15*, pp. 417-427.

103. D. Hall and E. Lawler, «Job Characteristics and Pressures and the Organizational Integration of Professionals,» *Administrative Science Quarterly*, 1970, *15*, pp. 271-281.

would be obtained through the quality of his performance in the university would be affected by his perception of how the decision to determine if he deserves tenure is arrived at by objective guidelines. He must know the criteria that the university uses to determine who deserves tenure in the organization. Usually the professor qualifies for consideration for tenure after a period of one year of service at the institution. During this time the professor who is concerned with the possibility of getting tenure will watch the decisional process. This experience would be fundamental in the development of his perception of the guidelines that rule the decisional process. We postulate that his perception of how the degree of effort-reward probability will lead to the desired reward is affected by the degree of structure of the decisional process.

Another variable that would affect the perception of effort-reward-probability is the degree of trust that the professor has in the administration of the university. Let's assume that the professor was promised when he was hired by the university that he could have enough resources to do research, but eventually he found that the university did not keep its promise. This negative experience will decrease the professor's perception of effort-reward probability because he does not trust the administration of the university. He will work hard during the probational period and in the end find that the university does not give him the reward. We consider that the experience perceived by the professor in the decisional process to determine if some of his colleagues deserve the reward is fundamental. If the professor perceives that his colleagues deserve a promotion and the university does not promote them, he develops a distrustful perception of the whole process. Therefore, these experiences are determinants of the professor's perception of effort-reward probability.

Like trust and structure, the professor's perception that there is red tape at the university would affect the perception of the association of effort-reward probability with the degree of effort exerted at the university. Assume, for example, that the professor knows that one of the relevant criteria used to determine if the professor deserves a promotion is his improvement of his teaching methods. Even though the professor considers that using film strips and fixed projectors to teach his courses will increase the probability of improving the teaching method, he is not going to exert any effort to use these methods if he realizes that there is a great deal of red tape involved in getting the movies, the projector and the operator in order to use these teaching resources in his classes. Therefore, red tape will affect also the professor's perception of effort-reward-probability.

But organizational conditions can affect other aspects of the model as well as effort-reward-probabilities. As we showed above, the image that a professor has a high degree of self-determination still exists. Thus, academic freedom would be a good predictor of the behavior of the professors at the university. The perception of the influence of people outside upon the relevant decisions in the university, and the perception of participation in decision-making would also be good predictors of the behavior of the professor at the university.

It seems that these three variables have a significant impact upon the images of self-determination that the professor has. Let's assume that the organizational setting in which the study is conducted is a university where the administration has a great deal of control over the professor's behavior. There is a rumor that many classrooms have tape-recorders in order to determine if the professors make use of political persuasion. The professor does not have any way to complain about this situation. Let's assume also that the professor perceives that all the relevant appointments in the university are made by the politicians, and the professor does not have any participation in the decisional process. However, in such a university the professor may get tenure and promotions if he shows that he is exerting a great deal of effort on the job and his performance is considered good.

We hypothesize that the professor with strong feelings that the university must have a climate of academic freedom and participation would not consider attractive the possibility of getting promotions and tenure, and if he decided to stay at the university he would decrease his effort and the quality of his performance would consequently diminish.

In this example, even though there is a high degree of instrumentality in obtaining the rewards at the organization, the organizational setting is inadequate; therefore, the path-goal model of work behavior alone is not able to explain the behavior of the professor observed in a setting such as the organizational setting that we described above.

This situation would be useful in explaining why the professors, even though they obtain the rewards offered by the organization, would still feel dissatisfaction with the university. In other words, the perception of academic freedom, the influence of the outsider in the relevant decisions at the university, and the feeling of participation in the relevant decisions at the university come between rewards and satisfaction in the path-goal model of work behavior.

The expectancy theory proposes that the rewards obtained by the individual may lead to satisfaction only when the individual perceives that the rewards he received were equitable. We propose that like the perception of equitable rewards, the feeling of academic freedom, the influence of outsiders in the decisional process, and the feeling of participation in the decisional process are intervening variables between rewards and satisfaction. In other words, even though the professor obtains rewards, these rewards are not going to produce satisfaction if the professor perceives that the university climate is inadequate for an academician because of the lack of freedom and respect for the professor's profession.

In summary, a professor may obtain promotions, tenure and many other rewards, but he is not going to experience satisfaction unless he perceives that the university setting fulfills him with academic freedom, participation in the decisional process, and that people outside the university do not control the relevant decisions. Of course, the proposition stated above assumes that the professor wants to participate and is concerned with academic freedom and the influence of outsiders in the decisional process at the university. When these are not important, then we would expect less dissatisfaction with the organization.

We did not mention above the perception that people outside the university have influence on the decisional process which may affect the professor's perception of effort-reward probability. We want to add some comments about that.

We assume that as with structure, trust and red tape, the feeling that the decisional process is influenced by people outside the university may be associated with the perception of effort-reward probabilities at the university. This is probably going to affect to a greater extent those professors who are really concerned with the possibility of becoming dean, chancellor or president of the university. If these decisions are affected to a great extent by the politicians, for example, the professor may have a lot of uncertainty. In addition, the degree of instrumentality is going to be down because the professor does not see any way to affect decisions through his performance. We hypothesize that this situation may produce a great deal of dissatisfaction in all professors who are really interested in reaching one of the positions at the top. Of course, in this example we are assuming that the appointment to a high position in the administration of the university is a desired reward and many professors want to pursue it.

As with the variables presented above, we consider that the

degree of warmth in the university and the degree of identification are related to the variables of the path-goal model. The "warmth climate" in the organization has been shown to be relevant in order to produce satisfaction. However, we hypothesize that the feeling that the organizational climate is warm is not enough to affect the degree of satisfaction experienced by the individual, but the fact that the professor gives importance to interpersonal relations and a friendly organizational climate would affect the value of the reward.

As Patchen stated, when an individual perceives that he derives, and expects to continue to derive, various satisfactions from his organization membership, he may support and defend this organization.[104] Therefore, if the individual perceives that his contribution is fundamental in order to maintain the organization in operation, his predisposition to exert high performance would increase. We propose that the degree of identification of the individual with the organization affects the amount of effort that he exerts in the organization.

Just as the perception that there are outsiders with power who affect the decisional process affects the way in which the value of the reward produces the amount of effort exerted by the professor, the perception that there are guidelines which structure the decisional process would affect the relationship stated by Porter and Lawler.

However, the perception that there are guidelines which rule the decisional process would affect the way that these variables predict effort in a different direction than the variable discussed above (the perception of influence by outsiders). We consider that this variable produces a different effect because the perception that outsiders may affect final decisions produces uncertainties, but the perception that the decisional process follows certain rules decreases the amount of uncertainty, increasing the instrumentality perceived by the professor. In other words, if the professor knows the rules that the university uses to determine whether he deserves tenure, promotion and other rewards, his perception of the instrumentality of his effort and performance will increase. Therefore, we propose that the job effort model would better predict the amount of effort exerted by a professor when he perceives that the decisional process is structured by certain guidelines or rules.

---

104. Martin Patchen, *op. cit.*, pp. 155-159.

THE ORGANIZATIONAL SETTING AS AN ALTERNATIVE EXPLANATION OF WORK BEHAVIOR

We have proposed how the variables in the organizational setting would affect Porter and Lawler's model of the individual's work behavior. However, the organizational setting would be an alternative explanation of the behavior observed by the individual in the organization. The model proposed by Porter and Lawler states that the value of the reward times the perceived effort-reward probability will lead to effort. The model also proposes that effort, ability, and role perception combine in order to produce individual performance. An alternative explanation would be that academic freedom, identification, structure and the perception of outsider power in the university's decisional process will explain greater variability in the individual's performance and effort than the combination of variables proposed by the expectancy theory.

As we discussed above, these organizational variables have been shown to be associated with performance and satisfaction in a significant way in many studies done in the field or organizational behavior. Therefore, it is possible that these variables alone have the power to predict the individual behavior at work to the same extent or better than the expectancy model proposed by Porter and Lawler.

This proposition assumes that there are individual attitudes toward the organization with power to predict the individual's behavior at work. Of course this is an alternative approach to explaining the individual's behavior at work. Much research following this line of thought is needed.

The approach presented here is not new. Already other researchers have seen the necessity of finding explanations for the individual work behavior other than the explanations proposed by the expectancy theory. John Turney concluded that "expectancy theory research has demonstrated that employee estimates of the likelihood that their work behavior leads to various desirable and undesirable outcomes is related to performance motivation. While the correlations between various expectancy constructs and measures of performance motivation are usually significant, more than half of the variance remains unexplained. Error variance attenuates the relationship to some extent. However, it is likely that a sizeable portion of the remaining variance can be attributed to variables which are not included within the basic expectancy model." [105]

Turney said that his proposition has found support in a number of recent reviews of research testing the basic expectancy model in the organizational setting, in which the authors have called for researchers in the area to consider other critical variables in addition to the expectancy formulation which relates to performance motivation (one of the literature reviews that Turney mentioned was Heneman and Schwab, cited previously in this study).

In fact, Turney's study showed that "the intrinsic value of the activity (employee simply enjoys performing an activity for its own sake or as an end in itself rather than as a means to other ends) was a much more useful predictor of motivation to perform an activity when compared with a measure of intrinsic value of the activity in a research and development lab." [106]

Therefore, it seems important to examine the direct effect these organizational conditions have on performance and satisfaction as alternative explanations to the path-goal model.

The fact that Turney's study was conducted among professionals in a research and development laboratory and our research was conducted among professors at universities is another reason to support our proposition and the necessity of the study. The results may show that the behavior of the professional at work can be explained by different models than for other types of workers at a job, because the professional may be more motivated by intrinsic rewards than other types of workers. Turney explains that the behavior of the professional in relation to the value of the activity itself is different from other types of worker behavior (such as factory workers) because the work is not seen as an instrumental means to other ends.

The proposition that the organizational setting would be an alternative explanation to the behavior of the individual at work adds a useful and valuable dimension to our study.

THE UNIVERSITY SETTING AND THE PATH-GOAL MODEL

The fact that the research setting of this study is the university required that we point out some conditions that might affect the

105. John R. Turney, «Activity Outcome Expectancies and Intrinsic Activity Values as Predictors of Several Motivation Indexes for Technical-Professionals,» *Organizational Behavior and Human Performance*, 1974, *11*, 65-82, p. 65.
106. *Ibid.*, p. 77.

results of Porter and Lawler's model of motivation. For example, the model proposes that in order for the expectancy theory to be useful in explaining and predicting the individual's work behavior, the individual must see that the desired rewards are determined through his performance in the organization. This condition is not fully met in the university setting because the increase in the salary of the professors is determined on a group basis. In other words, all the instructors receive the same increment in their salary, all the assistant professors receive a little more than the instructors, and so forth. This means that the individual's performance is not considered in determining who deserves a raise.

However, the decisions regarding promotion and which professors deserve to have a leave of absence to study or a sabbatical leave are determined through the professor's performance.

This situation may affect the perception of instrumentality of the professors at the university. However, if the professorial position produced motivation itself it would compensate for this limitation.

Another situation that must affect the expectancy model when the study is conducted in a university is the fact that the type of job that the professor has does not require him to be under supervision the whole day. The major part of the professorial job is done outside the professor's office; therefore, the chairman's evaluation is not quite adequate. Hence, the results of the job effort and job performance model would be affected by this situation. The chairman's evaluation of the professor's performance would not necessarily be the best way to determine the professor's performance.

The Porter and Lawler model also states that the subordinate role perception and the superior role expectation must be accurate in order that the individual's performance be considered appropriate or effective by the superior. The fact that professors and the chairman are professionals with similar experience, education, and knowledge or capabilities increases the probability that each define the professorial job in a different way. Then the degree of role accuracy would be low. This situation may cause the difference between the chairman's rating of the professor's effort and performance and the professor's own rating.

We considered that in the interpretation of the results obtained in this study these aspects must be taken into account.

THE UNIVERSITY SETTING AND ORGANIZATIONAL ATTITUDES AND STRUCTURES

The university setting must have an impact on some organizational attitudes also. In other words, perception such as participation in the decisional process, academic freedom, and perception that outsiders have strong influence in the decisional process may have a different impact when they are analyzed in the university than when they are considered in a setting like a company.

As we said before, the feeling of self-determination seems to be associated with the images the professor has of his university. Then we postulated that the lack of academic freedom or autonomy would produce a stronger impact on the behavior of the professor than a similar task constraint would have on the behavior of a company worker. This limitation could be perceived as an attempt to hurt the professor's self-esteem. As a matter of fact, one of the great attractions of being a professor would be the degree of self determination that the professorial position provides.

Another variable which might be particularly relevant in the university setting would be the perception of self-actualization. As we said already, the professorial job must be rich in intrinsic rewards. If the job does not permit the self-actualization of the professor, it would not be attractive any longer and the impact of that fact upon the professor's behavior would be greater than the perception of lack of self-actualization of a worker of a production company, at a lower level.

WORKING HYPOTHESES

1. The Elaborated Path-Goal Model

As we stated already the general hypothesis of this study is that the professor's performance in the university is a function of the following variables: value of reward, perceived effort-reward probability, effort, role perception, organizational role expectation, rewards (intrinsic and extrinsic), perceived equitable rewards, satisfaction and several organizational setting variables, such as academic freedom and identification, among others.

These variables constitute the Porter and Lawler's model of work behavior and the organizational setting variables that we considered relevant in order to improve our understanding of the behavior of the professors at the university.

The model of Porter and Lawler states that one's behavior can be predicted from (1) the probability of the behavior leading to various outcomes weighted by (2) the evaluation of those outcomes.

As Mitchell and Pollard imply,[107] this model should be divided in two sub-models: the job effort model and the job performance model. Porter and Lawler stated that effort is distinctly different from performance and a different model should be used to predict performance.

a. *The Relationship Between Reward Expectancies and Effort*

The job effort model would be considered the base of the path-goal model, because it is stated that the effort exerted in the organization is a function of the value of the reward times the effort-reward probability.

This model has been tested in many studies: some of them produced findings that supported the propositions of the model, but many others did not support the job effort model.

In this study two versions of the model will be tested: a multiplicative model and an additive one. So far, some studies support the theory that variables combine in a multiplicative way to predict effort, and others do not.

For example, Mitchell and Pollard found that both the multiplicative and the additive models successfully predicted effort but neither was clearly superior to the other.[108]

Lawler and Suttle also found support for the job effort model. However, the correlation coefficients were low and the results did not show that the variables combined in a multiplicative way to produce effort.[109]

Usually the models have been tested using more than one measurement of effort; and the results in some studies support the expectancy theory when one of the indexes is considered, and produce non significant results when other indexes of effort are used with the same data. For example, Pritchard and Sanders testing the job effort model found that the model predicted self

---

107. T. Mitchell and William Pollard, «Effort, Ability, and Role Perceptions as Predictors of Job Performance,» University of Washington, Seattle, Washington, 1973.

108. Mitchell and Pollard, *op. cit.*, p. 1.

109. Lawler and Suttle, *op. cit.*, pp. 17-18.

reported effort fairly well, but correlations with supervisory rating of effort were lower.[110]

It seems that so far we don't have conclusive results about the way in which the variables combine to produce effort, and whether the job effort model really predicts the amount of effort exerted by the individual in the organization.

Another important fact that we have to consider is that so far the model has been tested with only one motivator: pay. Probably the reason is the difficulty in measuring rewards other than pay. As Lawler said, pay in contrast to many rewards is measurable and thus lends itself rather easily to quantitatively oriented research.[111]

For example, Porter and Lawler in their study in 1968 tested the job effort model using pay as a satisfier. They did not consider any other motivator.[112]

Schuster *et al.* tested portions of the Porter and Lawler model regarding the motivational role of pay and of course the only motivator used was pay.[113]

Lawler and Suttle used 38 items to determine the perception of instrumentality of their subjects, but the question was based upon the probability of getting pay.[114]

Other researchers such as Mitchell and Pollard just used an index of effort ranked by the individuals themselves and their superiors.[115]

It seems that this study provides us the opportunity to see the effect of rewards other than pay in the behavior of the subjects. We assume that the professors at the university are not motivated only by their salary. As a matter of fact we expect that the best motivator in the university would be the intrinsic rewards. This proposition is based upon many studies which show that the professors mostly want to satisfy their higher order needs. For example Hagstom in 1965 concluded that the basis of scientist organization

110. R. Pritchard and M. Sanders, «The Influence of Valence, Instrumentality, and Expectancy on Effort and Performance,» *Journal of Applied Psychology*, 1973, 57, 55-60, p. 59.

111. Edward Lawler, *Pay and Organizational Effectiveness: A Psychological View*, New York, McGraw-Hill Co., 1971.

112. Porter and Lawler, *op. cit.*, p. 70.

113. Jay R. Schuster *et al.*, «Testing Portions of Porter and Lawler Model Regarding the Motivational Role of Pay,» *Journal of Applied Psychology*, 1971, 55, pp. 187-195.

114. Lawler and Suttle, *op. cit.*, p. 8.

115. Mitchell and Pollard, *op. cit.*, p. 4.

may be regarded as the exchange of social recognition for information.[116]

As we said above, the capacity of the professor to auto-determine his activities at the university is quite important in the academic life, therefore other needs than extrinsic needs may be motivators of the professor's behavior at the university.

We assumed that if we want to consider all the possible motivators of the professors at the university the best method to use is a scale which measures the degree of attractivenes of all the basic needs proposed by Maslow in 1954.[117] Hence, we used motivators which would fulfill the higher and lower needs: security, social, self-esteem, autonomy, and self-actualization.

The fact that not many studies have considered motivators rather than pay, and the fact that so far the research done has not provided conclusive results about the way in which the value of the reward times the perception of effort-reward probability combine to produce effort constitutes relevant reason to test the following hypothesis:

> A-1. *The higher the perceived probability that the rewards considered attractive by the professors depend on their effort, the greater the amount of effort that a professor will exert at the university.*

Porter and Lawler's model states that the combination of the value of reward times the perception of effort-reward probability predicts the amount of effort that the individual will exert at work. In this model the importance of the reward is critical in inducing the individual to start an action. However, there are other approaches that can be useful to get a deeper understanding of why individuals are motivated to start any action. For example, there is the question of which is the strongest predictor of individual action: the importance of the reward or the feeling of lack of rewards.

Another question is which type of rewards are better motivators of the professor's behavior at the university. This question is related to the effect of satiation of the need in the individual's behavior. In other words, what happens when the professors fulfill their needs? It is quite an important question because it is fundamental in the designing of the rewarding process by the univer-

---

116. Quoted by S. Blume and R. Sinclair in «Chemist in British Universities: A Study of the Reward System in Science,» *American Sociological Review*, 1967, 32, 391-407, p. 127.

117. A. Maslow, *Motivation and Personality*, New York, Harper, 1954.

sity. Maslow's theory said that "needs cease to play an active determining or organizing role as soon as they are gratified." [118] For example the professor who has been granted tenure is no longer motivated by this reward. This is of course more true of extrinsic than intrinsic rewards, which are relatively insatiable.

Alderfer, testing this theory of Maslow found that "when relatedness needs (safety impersonal, love belongingness, and esteem-interpersonal) are relatively dissatisfied, the less relatedness needs are satisfied, the more they will be desired; when relatedness needs are relatively satisfied, the more relatedness needs are satisfied, the more they will be desired. When both relatedness and growth needs (esteem-self, confirmation and self actualization) are relatively satisfied, the more relatedness needs are satisfied, the more growth needs will be desired. When growth needs are relatively dissatisfied, the less growth needs are satisfied, the more they will be desired; when growth needs are relatively satisfied, the more growth needs are satisfied, the more they will be desired." [119] Therefore, he concluded that "providing an incentive system which allowed a person to satisfy his needs which diminished in desirability with increased satisfaction would contain the roots of destruction of the incentive system. However, providing an incentive system which allowed a person to satisfy needs which increased in desirability with increased satisfaction would strengthen the incentive system." [120]

In other words, the decision to design the incentive system must take into account which rewards after being satisfied will still motivate the professors. Unfortunately in this research we cannot provide this information. However, we can analyze the first question: Which of the variables "value of reward" or the feeling of lack of reward is a better predictor of the amount of effort exerted by the professors at the university.

As we said before, many studies failed to find a significant relation between the value of the rewards times perceived effort-reward probability with effort. We considered that the measurement of effort used to test the model is quite important. Usually the studies used many indexes to measure effort: the individual self rating, the superior's rating, the peer rating, and objective

118. A. Maslow, «A Theory of Human Motivation,» *Psychological Review*, 1943, *50*, 370-396, p. 393.

119. Clayton P. Alderfer, *Existence, Relatedness, and Growth: Human Needs in Organizational Settings*, New York, The Free Press, 1972, p. 149.

120. *Ibid.*, p. 162.

measures of effort such as publications when the research is conducted in the academic setting.

In our study only two measurements of effort were used: the professor's self rating and the chairman's rating. Even though some estudies conducted in the university setting used the number of articles published in professional journals as an index of the amount of effort exerted by the professors, in our study we cannot use this measure because a publishing policy is not strongly followed by the professors at the University of Puerto Rico.

We considered appropriate the use of the self rating measure of effort to test how the value of the reward combines with perception of effort reward probability to predict effort because the path-goal model is intrapersonal, therefore the professor's perception of importance of the rewards times the degree of instrumentality of their performance might be associated with the professor's self rating of effort rather than with the chairman's measure of effort. What we wanted to test is if the professor's perception that an attractive reward depends on his performance induces him in his own mind to exert effort.

b. *The Relationship Between Effort, Role Perceptions and Performance Evaluations*

However, it is the organization which will determine whether the amount of effort and the level of performance of the worker is adequate. It is presumed that positively evaluated efforts will produce positively evaluated performances, subject only to the constraints of ability and role perceptions. In other words, for the purposes of this study, the effort-performance relationship will correlate well unless there is a significant discrepancy between the professor's and chairman's perceptions of the professor's role.

Therefore we hypothesize that:

> A-2, *The greater the effort the professor exerts (chairman rated), the higher the rating of his performance, subject to the accuracy of the professor's role perceptions.*

Porter and Lawler emphasize the fact that the appropriateness of an individual's role perception has an important influence on his job performance. However, as we said already, their model (and the models that tried to test their model) does not attempt to specify what the correct role perception is likely to be in a given situation.

We propose to determine in a more specific way how the role perception affects performance. We want to analize which conditions are appropriate in order that role perception can produce relevant performance. Then a method to measure the degree of role accuracy is going to be used which is based on the mean differences between the professor's role perception and the chairman's role expectation (this method was discussed in the section that presented the theoretical model).

We propose that even though the professor sees the relation between reward and performance, and has the ability necessary to do a good job and to exert high effort to perform his job effectively, his performance is not going to be ranked high by the chairman unless the chairman perceives that the professor is engaged in the activities that he considers adequate in order to produce a relevant performance. Then, we conclude that the degree of role accuracy is fundamental in order for the professor's performance to be considered effective.

It should be noted that in this proposition we are considering the chairman measures of effort and performance. The reason is that we are interested in determining the factors which explain the chairman's evaluation of the professor's performance.

Another fact that we have to point out is that even though the Porter and Lawler model includes the variable ability, in this study we are not measuring this variable. There is, of course, a growing literature in the assessment of professional performance and the ability of the professional has been measured several times. For example Mitchell and Pollard used two indexes of ability in their research among university professors: self rating of ability and peer rating of ability. Each professor listed the group of professors with whom he interacted closely and frequently in the conduct of his professional activities (peer rating of ability). They also were asked about their evaluation of their own ability (self rating of ability).[121] However they found almost all the coefficients of ability insignificant when they were associated with performance.

Lawler and Suttle used the Thurstone Test of Mental Alertness to measure the abilitty of the managers who constituted their subjects and also did not find that ability was a useful predictor. They found that the ability measures produced relatively low correlation with performance.[122]

---

121. Terence Mitchell and Pollard, *op. cit.*, p. 5.
122. Lawler and Suttle, *op. cit.*, p. 18.

We considered that we are not able to use any measurement of ability that allows us to establish an independent variable as to professional ability. As a matter of fact the professors at the University of Puerto Rico were reluctant to answer a questionnaire, hence it could be impossible to get their approval to measure their ability.

Some of the research findings reported already are useful to support the proposition A-2. As we mentioned before, Wall and Adams in their study of some variables affecting the evaluation of salesmen found the "the favorableness of the evaluation of the salesman's performance corresponded markedly to his obedience to the subject's first directive. Subjects receiving report of a salesman's obedience evaluated their salesman's performance most positively, and those who felt they had been disobeyed evaluated the performance most negatively.[123]

House and Rizzo in a recent study found that role conflict and role ambiguity were negatively correlated with perception of organizational effectiveness and satisfaction and positively correlated with anxiety, and member propensity to leave the organization.[124]

It seems that the degree of role accuracy plays a significant function in the production of relevant performance. However, the hypothesis proposes that the combination of effort times the degree of role accuracy is necessary in order to determine performance.

As in the case of the job effort model, the job performance model has been tested in many studies. As a matter of fact, all the studies tested both models because effort is one of the predictors of performance, and of course, the dependent variable of the path-goal model of work behavior is performance.

Porter and Lawler did not collect much information about ability when they tested the model in 1968. However, according to them, the model indicates that each of the predictors (effort, abilities, and role perceptions) should have an impact on performance, and that in combination they determine performance. They concluded, "Thus, not only is the notion of a combined effect of effort and role perceptions on performance supported, but also the results indicate the relationship may well be an interactive one. In other words, if extremely high effort were to combine with extremely inaccurate role perceptions, the prediction would

123. Wall and Adams, op. cit., p. 402.
124. House and Rizzo, op. cit., p. 496.

be that the subsequent performance would be evaluated as relatively ineffective." [125]

Mitchell and Nebeker tested the job performance model proposed by Porter and Lawler in 1968 using undergraduate students as their subjects. They concluded that "no difference can be found between the additive and multiplicative model in predicting performance in the setting in which the study was conducted. The measures of effort are not related to performance in the academic setting. Since measures of ability may already include elements of effort, and our measures of effort were not found to be strongly related to performance, the present job performance models may be inappropriate for the academic setting." [126]

Mitchell and Albright did not find support for the job performance and effort models. According to them the weighting of the sum of ability times the perceived instrumentality of successful performance for the attainment of outcome by effort did not significantly predict effort and performance.[127]

This study of Mitchell and Albright did not include role perception as a predictor of performance and assumed that effort leads directly to performance. The authors argued that the results of the study are confusing, but reviews of the previous work with this model provide little help in explaining their results because the research which has used the variable in the manner prescribed by the theory (they named Graen, 1969 and Arveyand Dunnette, 1970) has also obtained conflicting results.

Mitchel and Albright, as well as Heneman and Schwab (cited already), considered that the studies conducted so far were inadequate in testing the expectancy model and this adds another reason to test this model again through a more accurate measure of role perception as we are going to do.

Pritchard and De Leo did not find support for the Porter and Lawler model either. Neither did the variables predict individual performance in a significant way, nor was the multiplicative or additive pattern of interaction of the variables significant.[128]

---

125. Porter and Lawler, op. cit., p. 161.
126. Terence Mitchell and Nebeker, «Expectancy Theory Predictions of Academic Effort and Performance,» Journal of Applied Psychology, 1973, 57, 6-67, p. 66.
127. Terence Mitchell and Donald Albright, «Expectancy Theory Predictions of the Satisfaction, Effort, Performance, and Retention of Naval Aviation Officers,» Organizational Behavior and Human Performance, 1972, 8, 1-20, p. 15.
128. Pritchard and De Leo, op. cit., p. 267.

We, of course, as with hypothesis A-1, wish to determine whether the relationship between these variables is additive or multiplicative.

We have to point out that our measurement of role accuracy is determined by the professor's role definition and the chairman's perception of how the professor's roles should be defined. We assume that the chairman is the primary evaluator of the activities of the professor. Of course, it is not always true, when the professor's activities move out of the boundary of the department the opinion of other people must be significant in the definition of the professor's role. For example a professor who is really involved in the activities of a professional organization such as the Puerto Rican Association of University Professors may develop a different role perception than a professor who has just the co-workers of the department as a reference group.

c. *Determinants, Role Perceptions*

Our hypothesis A-1 proposes that the combination of the value of the reward and the perceived effort-reward probability explains the function of effort (self-rating). We considered that this combination also is important to determine the degree of role accuracy between the professors and the chairman.

We assumed that the professors are aware that the chairman is the person who is going to evaluate their activities in order to determine if they deserve the university's rewards such as tenure and promotion. Hence, the professors who are interested in obtaining these rewards conferred by the university are going to engage in the activities that the chairman considered appropriate in order to deserve a reward.

Therefore, we propose the following:

A-3.1 *The degree of role accuracy is a function of the value of the reward times the effort-reward probability.*

Some studies conducted in the literature will support the proposition that if the subordinate wants to get the organizational rewards he must behave according to expectations of his superiors. For example, Walton and McKersie found that in a negotiation when the representative of the group follows the method considered adequate by the group to pursue its objectives, even if he fails to get what the group wants, its members are not going to blame him.[129]

Wall and Adams found that salesmen (the subjects) thought to be obedient were evaluated more positively, granted more autonomy, and trusted more.[130] We assume that the chairman has a great deal of influence over the professor, who perceives that the chairman plays a fundamental role in the determination of the university's rewards, and considers that such rewards are attractive enough to induce him to work. The amount of influence that the chairman may have over the professor's behavior would be explained through the theory of social influence stated by Raven.[131] According to him, a person may influence the behavior of others through many sources of power, among which are coercive power, reward power, and expertise. From Raven's theory we can infer that the person with the strongest influence over the behavior of others would be the one who has the greater combination of powers in the environment in which the focal person interacts.

As we said already, we consider that the chairman, among all the people who interact with the professor, is the person who might have a unique combination of coercive, reward, and expert power to bring to bear on his influence attempts. His evaluation is fundamental in order to decide if the professor deserves the reward; he assigns the courses, the time schedules, etc. He might have expert power also if he has enough ability and knowledge to deserve this power. Therefore the chairman may have a great deal of influence over the behavior of the professors who consider the organizational reward attractive.

Another theory that supports our proposition is the theory of Stinchcombe.[132] As we said in the first part of this chapter, the Stinchcombe theory proposes that the effect of someone else's activity on the action and attitude of a person is a function of the probability that this person will pay attention to it, times the duration that the focal persons focuses his attention on the person who is going to exert the influence.

Assuming that the opinion of the chairman is quite important to the professor, the chairman may be very much able to influence

129. R. E. Walton and R. B. MacKersie, *A Behavior Theory of Labor Negotiations*, New York, McGraw-Hill, 1965.
130. James Wall, Jr. and J. Adams, «Some Variables Affecting a Constituent's Evaluations of Behavior Toward a Boundary Role Occupant,» *Organizational Behavior and Human Performance*, 1974, *11*, 390-408, p. 406.
131. Bertram Raven, *op. cit.*, pp. 371-382.
132. Stinchcombe, *op. cit.*, p. 236.

the professor's behavior because of the great deal of interaction between both almost every day at the university.

Following this line of thought we propose:

A-3.2 *The greater the relevance that the professor ascribes to the chairman's opinions about the way to define the professor's roles, and the more frequently that he interacts with the chairman, the greater will be the professor's agreement with the chairman's definition of the roles of the professor in the university.*

d. *The Relationship between Performance, Satisfaction and Equity*

In addition to the individual's effort and performance, the Porter and Lawler model of work behavior attempts to predict the degree of satisfaction experienced by the individual in the organization. The model tries to shed light on one of the issues that has produced much debate in the literature of industrial psychology. So far the question has been: what is the relationship between satisfaction and performance? Does satisfaction lead to performance or does performance lead to satisfaction?

Porter and Lawler's model proposes that satisfaction is a product of performance. According to them, differential performance determines differential rewards, which in turn produces differential satisfactions. Thus satisfaction is considered to be a function of performance-related rewards. The individual must feel satisfaction if he obtains a reward that meets or exceeds his needs. If in the organization the rewards are determined by the individual's performance, then the variability in the individuals' performances will explain the variability of the degree of satisfaction experienced by the individuals in the organization. They said that "if actual extrinsic rewards are given more or less in proportion to actual differences in performance, then perceptions of fulfillment should be related to performance differences. Perception of fulfillment, according to the model, does not, however, lead directly to satisfaction. The relation between fulfillment and satisfaction is modified by the individual's level of perceived equitable rewards, in that satisfaction is conceived as the difference between perceived equitable and actual rewards." [133]

Some important points of this theory must be considered. First,

---

133. Porter and Lawler, *op. cit.*, p. 162.

performance leads to satisfaction only when the organizational rewards are a function of performance. In other words, if in the university the rewards are not contingent with the professor's performance, performance does not lead to satisfaction.

The relationship between performance and satisfaction would never be perfect because in addition to the extrinsic rewards the individual is satisfied by intrinsic rewards. These intrinsic rewards are provided by the individual himself; therefore, performance evaluation does not necessarily affect the attainment of this type of reward.

If our proposition about the types of rewards that satisfy the professor is correct, the relationship between performance and satisfaction would be weak because we assume that the best motivators of a professor at the university are the intrinsic rewards.

Another aspect that is important to point out is: the perception that the reward obtained is equitable is fundamental in producing satisfaction. If the professor receives a reward such as promotion or tenure, but he perceives that other professors who also got promotion or tenure did not deserve them, he would not be satisfied with his reward.

The data that we collected would be useful in testing this proposition presented by Porter and Lawler. Assuming that the rewards in the university are determined by the performance of the professor, we can hypothesize that:

A-4.1 *The higher the professor's performance, the greater his satisfaction, assuming that he perceived that the rewards that he attained were equitable.*

We must point out that the method of developing data adopted in this study, since it is not time sensitive, raises serious doubts about establishing this aspect of the model. Nevertheless, a positive correlation between performance and satisfaction, assuming that the perceived equitable reward is an intervening variable, may provide some support for the model proposed by Porter and Lawler.

Also, we have to explain that the sense of inequity is cumulative and broader than the specific path-goal theory on which Porter and Lawler's model is based. In effect, equity or perceived equitable rewards is an intervening variable between the feeling of being rewarded or the amount of reward obtained and the degree of satisfaction experienced. But also many studies such as Pritchard's *et al.*,[134] and Telly *et al.*,[135] among others, used equity as an *alternative* explanation of satisfaction.

In the case of equity as a variable in the path-goal model the individual's satisfaction, from the point of view of the path-goal analysis, should not be treated as general satisfaction, but as specific satisfaction with the rewards received. The feeling of satisfaction is explained by the perception of being rewarded as a premium for producing performance considered meaningful by the organization.

We stated earlier that the chairman would consider that a professor is a high performer when he sees that the latter is engaged in the activities considered appropriate in order to produce relevant performance. If our assumption is correct and the rewards in the university are contingent to the professor's performance, the degree of role accuracy should explain the degree of satisfaction experienced by the professors at the university. The logic of this propositions is the following. If the professor's reward is determined by the chairman and the degree of role accuracy explains the evaluation of the professor's performance by the chairman, the degree of accuracy in role perception must be associated with the satisfaction that the professor experiences at the university (assuming that performance leads to satisfaction). The chairman ranks the professor's performance high; therefore, the professor obtains the rewards that satisfy him. We propose that the degree of role accuracy is associated with satisfaction because the professor's evaluation is affected by the degree of role accuracy. We propose the following:

A-4.2 *The degree of role accuracy between the chairman and the professor is associated with the satisfaction experienced by the professor.*

This proposition has some support in the studies conducted on role perception so far.

For example, Greene and Organ found that the relationship between performance and satisfaction is mediated by the compliance of the subordinate to his superiors. "Much recent research has investigated three related conditions of the received role—role

134. Robert Pritchard *et al.*, «Effects of Perception of Equity and Inequity on Worker Performance and Satisfaction,» *Journal of Applied Psychology*, 1972, *56*, pp. 75-94.

135. Charles S. Telly *et al.*, «The Relationship of Inequity to Turnover Among Hourly Workers,» *Administrative Science Quarterly*, 1971, *16*, pp. 164-172.

accuracy, clarity, and consensus—and almost all converge on the finding that these properties are associated with job satisfaction. The results further indicated that compliance, in turn, is a direct cause of satisfaction through its direct effect on performance evaluation." [136]

Kahn et al. found that role conflict and role ambiguity produce low job satisfaction. Their explanation is that this ambiguity is a source of tension and pressure that leads to dissatisfaction.[137]

Tosi found results consistent with Kahn's et al. findings. "The general tenor of the results presented is fairly consistent and supportive of Kahn's et al. research. These researchers concluded that the "emotional costs of role conflict (and role ambiguity) include low job satisfaction. The relationship between role conflict and job satisfaction was in the predicted direction ($r = -.37$). Lower levels of role conflict were associated with higher levels of job satisfaction. Role ambiguity, however, was not significantly related to job satisfaction." [138]

Lyons found that nurses with a high need for role clarity were dissatisfied when the degree of role clarity in the hospital was low.[139]

Rizzo, et al., found that role conflict and ambiguity correlated in a significant way with organizational member anxiety, satisfaction, and propensity to leave the organization. "The overall negative correlations indicate lowered degrees of need fulfillment with increased role conflict and role ambiguity." [140]

We consider that these studies are fairly consistent with the hypothesis that there is an association between role perception and satisfaction. Whether the explanation of this association is that the lack of role accuracy induces the superior to evaluate low the subordinate performance and decrease the rewards received by him, or that role conflict produces tension and therefore dissatisfaction, these studies support to some extent our proposition.

---

136. Greene and Organ, op. cit., p. 102.
137. Kahn et al., op. cit., p. 86.
138. Henry Tosi, op. cit., p. 18.
139. Thomas Lyons, «Role Clarity, Need for Clarity, Satisfaction, Tension, and Withdrawal,» Organizational Behavior and Human Performance, 1971, 6, pp. 99-110.
140. Rizzo et al., «Role Conflict and Ambiguity in Complex Organizations,» Administrative Science Quarterly, 1970, 15, 150-163, p. 161.

2. Organizational Setting Hypotheses

a. *The Relationship Between Organizational Setting and Independent Variables of the Path-Goal Model*

Our theory discussion has suggested that the path-goal model elaborated by Porter and Lawler would be affected by the organizational setting. The individual's attitudes and expectations would be significantly related to organizational conditions over and above those proposed by the expectancy theory of motivation.

One of our assumptions is that these conditions of the organizational setting may affect to some extent the expectation of the individual and, therefore, the outcomes proposed by Porter and Lawler. Another possibility is that these conditions not only affect expectancy but other variables of the elaborated path-goal model.

There are three types of organizational conditions which seem particularly relevant to the working behavior of the professor. The first of these, which is often treated in the literature, is participation in decision-making. This includes both the general concept of participation in the decision concerning job related activities. The second of these is the structuring of organizational activities, in this case, red tape. And the third, again often treated in the literature, is the affective climate of the organization: such factors as trust, equity, identification and warmth. We shall take these up in order, in this section hypothesizing their effects on the independent variables of the path-goal model and in the next section their effects on the dependent variables of the path-goal model.

While it is not obvious theoretically how these variables will affect the model, some do have rather obvious connections with specific variables. It will be necessary for our data analysis not only to test these connections but to explore other connections.

As has been argued, the relation between the value of the reward times the perceived effort-reward probability and effort is the basis of the Porter and Lawler model. If the individual does not exert effort, he will not produce performance because the individual's effort is one of the determinants of his performance.

In this relationship, the value of the reward is fundamental because if the individual does not consider the reward attractive he will not exert any effort in order to get it.

If the assumption that academic freedom must exert a strong impact on the behavior of the professor is correct, we will propose that the value of other rewards is affected by the lack of academic freedom. We assume that a professor who considers that academic freedom is a fundamental characteristic of the university environment would rank low the value of other rewards when he perceives a lack of academic freedom. We consider that this proposition has strong support in the university setting because many of the professor's rewards are intrinsic: satisfaction of self-actualization needs, self-esteem, autonomy, and so forth.

If the feeling of academic freedom is associated with the value of reward, the university's rewards are unattractive when the professor feels a lack of academic freedom, and the whole equation in the path-goal model which produces effort would be affected. Because the base of this equation is the value of the reward, if the professor does not consider the reward attractive he is not going to exert any effort in order to attain this reward.

Over and above the general concept of academic freedom, there is the question as to what extent the professor perceives himself as free to participate in a variety of academic activities, from faculty recruitment to student admissions. And in the case of the Universities of Puerto Rico there is the relevant issue of whether or not the faculty perceives a strong outsider role in the determination of these activities in the university. Participation in these activities should, as is the case with academic freedom, affect the professor's sense of his instrumentality. This heightened (or lowered) sense of instrumentality may well modify his perception of the probabilities that his efforts will produce rewards.

Structuring Activities. Two notions of structuring of activities seem of particular concern to the professors in the organizations under study. The first of these is red tape, the question of whether paper work or "bureaucratic" procedures inhibit the professor's attempts to perform his role. This factor could well affect the professor's sense of instrumentality. The second notion, that of the existence of guidelines or procedures for the carrying out of various activities, relates to the structural concept of formalization. This concept is not necessarily a negative concept as is red tape, inasmuch as guidelines and procedures may be facilitating more than obstructing for a variety of activities. We hypothesize, in fact, that guidelines and procedures would be positively correlated with the professor's sense of instrumentality.

The Affective Climate. The literature has consistently recognized three affective aspects of the organizational setting: trust; identification; warmth. A fourth affect (feelings of equity) has been introduced directly into the elaborated path-goal model by Porter and Lawler. The relationship of these variables to the expectancy model itself is not too clear. While the level of trust should have a definite effect on the professor's assessment that his efforts will produce rewards, it is not clear that identification and warmth should affect this variable. A warm, supportive atmosphere may encourage confidence, of course, but not clearly confidence as it is set in the expectancy model. Identification would seem to have little relation to the sense of instrumentality except in the opposite direction; namely instrumentality may affect the level of identification.

On the other hand we would expect to find that these affective aspects of the work setting may modify the importance of the rewards variable of the path-goal model in as much as positive levels of these variables may themselves be sources of need fulfillment. These may be sources of feelings of belonging which could modify the importance of a variety of other types of rewards.

In summary, we would hypothesize the following relationships between organizational condititons and the independent variables of the path-goal model:

B-1.1. *The importance of rewards will be affected by academic freedom, trust, equity, identification, and warmth.*

B-1.2. *Instrumentality (effort-reward probability) will be affected by academic freedom, participation in decisions, outsiders' influence on decisions, and trust.*

b. The Relationship Between Organizational Setting and the Dependent Variables of the Elaborated Path-Goal Model

The three dependent variables of the elaborated path-goal model are effort, performance and satisfaction. Again we would expect organizational conditions to vary in the significance of their relationships with these variables.

Participation in Decision making. There is much literature support for relating participation in decision-making to job satisfaction. We might further hypothesize that for a university the level of academic freedom might be a negative if not a positive factor in faculty morale. Only as morale (in this case, satisfaction) would in turn affect effort and performance would we hypothesize a relationship between these variables and participation.

Structuring of Activities. Red tape is by its definition a negative affect; consequently we would expect a relationship between this affect and satisfaction. So also, guidelines and procedures if facilitating could lead to satisfaction. Both also, however, may affect performance directly since they structure the processes of the work itself.

The Affective Climate. Equity has been hypothesized by Porter and Lawler and others as affecting satisfaction with rewards. There should also be a relationship between general satisfaction and identification and warmth. It is not clear whether trust will directly affect satisfaction. Only to the extent that these variables affect the general morale of the professor would we expect them to perhaps affect effort and performance. Whether these variables directly affect performance and effort should be determined by examining the data.

In summary, we would hypothesize the following relationships between organizational conditions and the dependent variables of the path-goal model:

B-2.1. *Satisfaction will be related to academic freedom, participation in decision making, outsiders' influences over decisions, red tape, structuring of activities with guidelines or procedures, equity, warmth, and identification.*

B-2.2. *Effort and performance will be related to red tape and structuring of activities by guidelines and procedures.*

B-2.3. *Satisfaction with rewards will be related to equity.*

III. THE RESEARCH METHODOLOGY

GENERAL RESEARCH DESIGN

The function of research design is to devise a strategy and procedures so that the results will lead to acceptance or rejection of the hypothesized relationships. As many researchers, we prefer to design a study such as an experimental study, which typically involves experimenter-reproduced changes in one variable in order to observe the effects on a second variable, by which we can analyze the causality of the different relationships.

However, for many reasons it is quite difficult to design such a study; therefore, we used a correlational study in order to test our model.

A correlational study focuses on the relationship between two variables without either of them being altered by the experimenter. The major disadvantage of this study is its inadequacy to prove directly the existence of cause and effect relationships that are specified in a conceptual model. However, a correlation study can establish whether two variables tend to be related at a fixed point in time. Like Porter and Lawler we consider that if a close relationship were found as predicted, it would offer some support for our model; however, it does not establish that a cause and effect relationship exists. On the other hand, if no relationship were to be found where the model predicts that one exists, then it is possible for a correlational study to discredit part of the model.

THE RESEARCH SITE

This study was conducted in five universities and colleges in Puerto Rico. Four of these universities and colleges are private, and the University of Puerto Rico is a State (or Government) University.

The University of Puerto Rico has about 50 thousand * students and three thousand professors. It was established in 1903 and offers associate, bachelor, master degrees, and Ph.D. degrees in some technical and liberal arts fields.

The University of Puerto Rico is a multi-campus system. The main campus is located in the metropolitan area of San Juan. It has 26 thousand students. The school of Engineering Science is located on the West coast of the island, with 10 or 12 thousand students. The School of Medicine and allied matters is located in the capital, San Juan. Four "Community Colleges" and two four-year colleges are spread throughout different towns on the island.

The Puerto Rico Junior College is a Community College that eventually was developed into a four-year college. It is a multi-campus system with eight thousand students and about 300 professors, located in the Metropolitan Area of San Juan. It is a private college under the administration of a board of trustees.

The Sagrado Corazón College is a Catholic University with four thousand students and two hundred professors. It is located in the Metropolitan Zone of San Juan.

The Regional College of the Catholic University of Puerto Rico is a small college located in a town toward the South of the island. It has about two thousand students and one hundred professors.

The Turabo College is a recent college established three years ago by the same board of trustees as the Puerto Rico Junior College. It is located in the middle-eastern part of the island. The Turabo College has about four hundred students and two hundred and fifty professors.

SAMPLE SIZE

A questionnaire (see Appendix I) was sent to 1500 professors from the five universities and colleges mentioned above. We did not use any random method to select the sample because many of the sample sites are small colleges and the whole faculty was included. On the main campus of the University of Puerto Rico and in its campus at Mayagüez not all the professors were in-

---

* All numerical data are those of the year 1973, when the field study was made.

cluded; however, we were careful to include representatives of all the academic areas. Table 3-1 shows that in every college of that University professors from Humanities, Social Sciences, Business Administration, Education, Natural Sciences, Engineering and Agriculture were included.

Two hundred and sixty three questionnaires (unanswered) were returned because the professors were on vacation, left the university, or for other reasons. After seven weeks we received 350 responses. That means that the level of return was 28 % of the questionnaires that we sent. However, the level of return from each university or college ranged from 13 % at Cayey to 80 % at the Catholic University, with the exception of the University of Turabo where only .06 % of the professors answered the questionnaires.

Table 3-1 shows that the representation of the different departments was good. In the academic field of Humanities the level of return ranged from .05 % to 33 % in all the universities included. The level of return in the area of Social Sciences ranged from 0 % to 28 %. The field of Business Administration was represented by a significant number of returned questionnaires in all the colleges. The level of return in the area of Education ranged from 0 % in some colleges to 50 %. The distribution in the field of Natural Sciences ranged from .05 % to 50 %. Only three colleges offer courses in engineering and related fields. The percentages of questionnaires returned in these colleges in the field of engineering were 33 %, 25 %, and 23 %. The field of agriculture was offered only in the University of Puerto Rico at Mayagüez and the percentage of questionnaires returned was 18 %.

Therefore, we concluded that even though the percentage of questionnaires returned was not high, every college *was represented* in the sample and every academic field had an *appropriate* representation. Nevertheless, we cannot escape the possible conclusion that there is perhaps a systematic bias in the non-responses to our survey and our conclusions should be considered in the light of this level of non-response. Moreover, the degree of generalizability of these research findings is also affected by the fact that the study was conducted in Puerto Rico. Hence, the influence of cultural aspects may affect the generalizability of the results obtained.

Table 3-1

Distribution of Questionnaires Back:
Per Universities and Departments Included

University	Percent Questionnaire Back	Departments Included						
		Humanities	Social Sciences	Business Administration	Education	Natural Sciences	Engineering	Agriculture
Colegio Universitario Sagrado Corazón	52 %	3 %	0 %	1 %	50 %	1 %	—	—
P. R. J. College	16 %	5 %	2 %	0 %	34 %	28 %	—	—
University of Puerto Rico								
U.P.R. at Humacao	65 %	60 %	—	—	—	50 %	—	—
U.P.R. at Aguadilla	25 %	30 %	0 %	33 %	0 %	1 %	—	—
U.P.R. at Río Piedras	15 %	15 %	14 %	27 %	14 %	12 %	—	—
U.P.R. at Bayamón	28 %	33 %	0 %	33 %	50 %	5 %	33 %	—
U.P.R. at Ponce	14 %	25 %	20 %	20 %	0 %	31 %	25 %	—
U.P.R. at Arecibo	33 %	25 %	28 %	28 %	66 %	27 %	—	—
U.P.R. at Cayey	13 %	1 %	22 %	0 %	.08 %	16 %	—	—
U.P.R. at Mayagüez	16 %	1 %	16 %	22 %	1 %	12 %	23 %	18 %
Catholic University at Guayama	80 %							
Turabo University	6 %							
TOTAL	28 %							

DESCRIPTION OF THE VARIABLES

The variables we measured through our questionnaire were the variables of the elaborated path-goal model and selected variables describing organizational conditions. These variables are as follows:

Leading: *Path-Goal Variables*

A. *Value of Reward* — This variable refers to the attractiveness of possible outcomes to individuals; in other words, how attractive or desirable is a potential outcome of an individual's behavior in the work situation.

B. *Effort-Reward Probability* — This variable refers to an individual's expectations concerning the likelihood that a given amount of reward depends upon a given amount of effort on his part. In other words, it refers to an individual's perception of whether differential rewards are based on differential amounts of effort on his part in the work situation.

C. *Effort* — This variable refers to the energy expended to perform some task, but *does not necessarily correlate with how successfully the task is carried out.* By effort, Porter and Lawler mean the amount of energy an individual expends in a given situation. Of course, by energy they do not mean simply muscular movement. It also refers to mental or intellectual effort.

D. *Performance* — This means how successful the role achievement of the professor is. It is essentially an evaluation of the performance by the organizational members.

E. *Role Perception* — This variable refers to the direction of effort, the kinds of activity and behavior the individual believes he should engage in to perform his job successfully. It deals with the way in which the individual defines his job and the types of effort he believes are essential to effective job performance.

F. *Role Expectations* — Refers to the perception of the organization's administration about the kind of activities and behavior that they consider individuals should engage in to perform their job successfully. This variable, combined with E should determine evaluation of performance.

G. *Rewards* — This item refers to desirable outcomes or returns to a person that are provided by himself or by others. Rewards are desirable states of affairs that a person receives from either his own behavior or the behavior of others.

H. *Perceived Equity as to Rewards* — This variable refers to the level or amount of reward that an individual feels he should receive as the result of a given level of performance. It can also refer to the amount of reward an individual feels should be attached to a particular position or job in the organization.

I. *Satisfaction* — This variable refers to the feelings of satisfaction the individual experiences with the rewards he receives in connection with his job.

Organizational Setting Variables

A. *Perception of Organizational Warmth* — This focuses on the feeling of general good fellowship that prevails in the work group atmosphere; the emphasis is on being accepted and the prevalence of friendly and informal social groups.

B. *Participation in Relevant Organizational Decision Making* — Focuses on the amount of involvement there is among all organizational members in having some input into decision making.

C. *Academic Freedom* — Based on the feeling that prevails concerning the freedom to express one's own opinion, perception of authority in the classroom, and freedom to design and teach the courses.

D. *Red Tape* — Focuses on the degree to which members of the organization feel that there are many rules, procedures, policies, and practices to which they have to conform rather than being able to do their work as they see fit.

E. *Trust* — Is defined as an action that (a) increases one's vulnerability (b) to another whose behavior is not under one's control, (c) in a situation in which the penalty one suffers if the other abuses that vulnerability is greater than the benefit one gains if the other does not abuse that vulnerability.

F. *Identification* — This variable refers to the individual's feeling that his organization satisfies his own needs and permits him to obtain his personal objectives. It is the attitude of an individual to support and defend an organization of which he is a member because he derives and expects to derives various satisfactions from his membership in the organization.

G. *Perception of Outsider Power* — This variable refers to the individual's perception that external forces have strong power in the relevant decisions of the organization.

H. *Structure* — Is defined as the individual's perception that the decisional process in the organization is structured by definite guidelines and regulations.

MEASUREMENTS

The variables presented in our model need to be operationalized if the relationships between the variables are to be tested. By operationalizing a concept we mean to specify exactly what the concept is and develop a means of measuring it.

We used the following method in order to operationalize the variable called "value of reward." The professor ranked or rated the value of different rewards to themselves on an attitude scaling device.

We used a version of the questionnaire that Porter and Lawler used in their research in 1968.

"Below, are listed a number of things that you can either do in your job or can receive from your job. For each such thing, you will be asked to give four ratings: (a) How much is there now? (b) How much would you like there to be? (c) How much do you consider that your personal effort can affect the amount that you will get in the future? (d) How important is this to you?"

"Each rating will be on a seven-point scale, which will look like this:

(minimum) 1 2 3 4 5 6 7 (maximum)

Question (d) "How important is this (referring to the reward) to you?" was used in order to measure the variable "value of reward."

The variable named "reward" was divided into two categories: extrinsic and intrinsic.

Following Maslow as well as Porter and Lawler, we consider that the indicators of this variable are the rewards that a person might hope to obtain in his job, such as: promotion, tenure, salary, self-actualization, self-esteem, etc.

As we said, "effort-reward probability" refers to an individual's perception of whether differential rewards are based on differential amounts of effort on his part in the work situation.

In order to operationalize this variable, a list of activities that concerns universities was derived. We consider that this activity or thing that the professor would obtain was the reward. We asked each professor his perception as to how his performance in these activities would lead to the gaining of these rewards. Question (c) in the example above was used to measure this variable: "How much do you consider that your personal effort can affect the amount (of the proposed reward) that you will get in the future?"

In other words, the indicators of this variable are the expectations of the professors that the job's rewards depend upon a given amount of effort in their professional activities. (See Appendix I for the questionnaire used.)

In this research the variable "effort" was measured by a self-report by the professors and a report by the chairman of the department. A seven-point scale was used in order to measure this variable (see appendix I).

The variable "performance" was also measured using both the evaluation by the chairman of the professors in his department and the professor's self-report. A seven-point scale was used to measure this variable.

The choice of measure of job performance and effort used in this study was largely determined by the topic of our research as was also the case in Porter and Lawler's study. Since we are measuring professors' attitudes and performance, many of the usual measures of job performance did not appear to be relevant. (In the case of "effort", this variable has not been used very often in research.)

The assumption was made that the chairman and the professor were both in a reasonable position to evaluate the professor's performance, since they both have adequate knowledge of the job and the job performance.

We used the same procedure to measure variables such as "identification," "academic freedom," "participation in decision-making," "red tape," and so forth.

As stated above, an individual must feel identification with the organization when he perceives that it will satisfy his needs and achieve his purpose. Therefore, we used the following indicators in order to operationalize the variable called "identification": support of organizational objectives, remaining in the organization, the feeling of personal need satisfaction, and the feeling of organization prestige. All these indicators were used by Patchen [1] in order to operationalize the concept of identification in the study that he conducted on the TVA.

We used the following indicators in order to operationalize the variable "academic freedom": freedom to participate in designing the curriculum of his department program, freedom to express his own opinion in the classroom, and freedom to choose textbooks and determine all matters about the academic features of his courses. We chose these indicators after a careful review of several books and articles which deal with the topic, such as the *Bulletin of the American Association of University Professors, Professors as Teachers*, published by Eble,[2] and *The Tenure Debate* by Smith,[3] among others.

The variable called "participation in decision making" was represented by the following indicators: participation in the establishment of new academic programs; participation in the decision of student admissions to his department; participation in the process of faculty recruitment; participation in the university's budget distribution; participation in the selection process of the university's administrators such as chairman, dean, chancellor, and president; and participation in curriculum changes. Based upon our experience, we thought that these decisions are considered relevant by the professors.

The variable called "perception of outsider influence" was operationalized by asking the professor about his perception of the degree of power or influence that people outside the university have in the decisions that were used as indicators of the "participation in decision making" variable.

Two indicators were used in order to operationalize the variable called "warmth": friendly atmosphere that prevails among the personnel of the university and adequate interpersonal relations at the university.

In addition to overall satisfaction, we measured a variable called "satisfaction" which was operationalized as a discrepancy, following Porter's approach.[4] He defines satisfaction as the difference between responses to a "How much is there now?" item and re-

---

1. Martin Patchen, *op. cit.*, p. 257.
2. Eble, *op. cit.*
3. Bardwell Smith and Associates, *The Tenure Debate*, California, Jossey Bass Publisher, 1973.
4. Lyman Porter, «A Study of Perceived Need Satisfaction in Bottom and Middle Management Jobs,» *Journal of Applied Psychology*, 1961, *45*, pp. 1-10.

sponses to a "How much should there be?" item. When these two items are asked for a number of job facets or needs, the differences between these two types of items is computed, and the differences are summed across job facets to yield a measure of overall satisfaction.

Facets

$$JS = \sum \text{importance X (should be } - \text{ is now)}$$

In the case of the variable called "organizational role expectation," we asked each chairman to rank the importance of each role or task of the faculty member. Using a five-point scale the chairman ranked each one of the sixteen tasks or roles that a professor should have in the university. The same sixteen roles were ranked by the professor in order to measure the variable named "role perception."

The measurement of both variables was complemented by asking both the professors and the chairman to report the percent of time that they consider a professor should spend in each of the following role activities: teaching, preparing their lesson, attending committee meetings, being available to counsel students, studying in their specialization (doing research, reading articles, taking courses, etc.) and working in administrative affairs. The respondents distributed 100 percentage points across the activities listed above.

Using the variables called "organizational role expectation" and "professor role perception," we constructed a new variable which measured the degree of disagreement or accuracy of role perception. The mean difference of both variables was used in order to construct the new variable. In order to avoid the negative sign each mean difference computed was squared and then the square root was computed. The product of this procedure was a mean difference between the professor role perception and the chairman role expectation. An index of the mean differences between both variables was constructed in each case. We have two sections in the questionnaire designed to measure the professor's role perception and the chairman's role expectation (that is, Sections II and V, 1); therefore, two indexes which measure the degree of accuracy of role perception were constructed. These indexes were converted as variables 201 (Section II) and 202 (Section V, 1) in the data analysis. The differences between the two are differences in attitudes as to activities (VAR 201) and differences in time spent on activities (VAR 202).

RELIABILITY AND VALIDITY OF SCALES

Our questionnaire was formed by many items and scales already tested in research conducted in the United States, such as the Porter scale to measure satisfaction, the Patchen scale to measure identification, and so forth. Since our research was conducted in Puerto Rico and the respondents were Spanish and English-speaking, we constructed two versions of the same questionnaire.

In order to secure the realiability and validity of the items, we followed these procedures. The first draft of the questionnaire was written in English, and worded in such a way as to make it meaningful to a university professor. Then, the questionnaire was translated into Spanish by a group of five bilingual graduate students who read both versions. Four of them are native Spanish speakers and the other is an English-speaking student. After corrections were made the English-speaking person read the English version and a Spanish-speaking professor read the Spanish version.

Even though this procedure seemed useful in translating the questionnaires, many questions could be misunderstood. Therefore the validity and reliability of this questionnaire could be affected by this limitation.

Another limitation of this questionnaire was the type of measure used. When measuring individual attitudes and perceptions there is the risk of getting many response biases. For example, there is the possibility that the subjects attempted to give socially desirable responses. Furthermore, even though the respondents were anonymous, it is possible that professors distorted answers in order to avoid any risk in case their answers were used to evaluate their performance by the administration of the university.

The amount of missing data was another problem in the study. Some questionnaires were incomplete in some sections because the professors did not understand the questions or did not want to provide the information. Fortunately, the SPSS program provides a method of handling the problem of missing data. The sections in which the subjects did not provide answers were dropped from the analysis.

Prior to the present study, a pilot questionnaire containing many items similar to those on the final questionnaire was administered to a small sample that included faculty from three universities which were in the sample of the final study.

The reliability and validity of the items on the pilot questionnaire were evaluated and utilized in constructing the questionnaire used in the final study. A program (ATSCALE) for the evaluation of the unidimensionality and internal consistency of scales was used in the construction of the scales.

This program included two traditional means used to determine if all items in a scale are tapping a common trait. According to Burns,[5] the first method is a simple summation of responses to each item, where the items have been keyed such that a higher value is equivalent to having more of the underlying attribute in question. The major criterion here for evaluating a scale is its internal consistency or homogeneity of items. Good items are those which have a high correlation with the other items in the scale and with the total score.

This program also considered the Guttman scale analysis. A person's pattern of responses to items is assumed to be reproducible from his total score. Any individual who responds positively to a particular item should also have responded positively to all items of greater popularity than that particular item. The major criterion for evaluating scales in this tradition is the extent of reproducibility of the pattern of responses to items from the total scores. The more exact the prediction of individual's scores, the higher the reproducibility of the scales.

The statistics in the program which measure reproducibility or homogeneity of dichotomous items are: Guttman's coefficient of reproducibility, comparison of chance, obtained and ideal expectancy of ideal scale types, Green B, Green Index of Consistency (B), Loevinger Index of Homogeneity, Kuder-Richardson Formula 20, corrected K-R 20, and inferred average inter-item correlation for K-R 20 and corrected K-R 20.

The program uses the Pearson Product-Moment Correlation coefficient to measure the linear association between items. A pattern of high correlation indicates the presence of a correspondence of positions, or reflects the possibility that all items are tapping the same underlying factor. A pattern of low or zero correlation indicates the presence of no relationship and, therefore, the pos-

---

5. John A. Burns, «A Manual to Accompany Program ATSCALE: Evaluation of the Unidimensionality and Internal Consistency of Responses to a Series of Questions,» Department of Psychology, Northwestern University, Evanston, Illinois, 1974.

sible presence of more than one factor with people having different relative positions across the dimensions or factors. Thus the corrected item-total correlations are a useful indicator of an item's relationship or association with the whole scale. Items with low or negative corrected item-total correlations should be dropped from the scale.

The Green Index is another statistic provided by the ATSCALE program. This index represents an approach to error counting in which what are counted are not the errors associated with any one individual, but the deviations from pairs of patterns of responses. According to Burns, the Green B index represents "an approximation to counting all combinations of errors that deviate from the ideal 01 pattern when items have been ordered in ascending popularity." [6] In other words, the Green B index becomes similar in form to Guttman's reproducibility coefficient.

The program also uses the Green Index of Consistency which is an approach to the analysis of the internal consistency of the scale.

Another approach to measure reproducibility of scales is provided by the ATSCALE program: the Loevinger Index of Homogeneity.

As Burns explains, "Loevinger derives the index by comparing every combination of pairs of items and calculating both the number of errors and the maximum possible number of errors given the item distributions. This gives this index and advantage over the Guttman coefficient of reproducibility which is sensitive to item distributions." [7]

The Kuder-Richardson Formula 20 represents a different approach than traditional Guttman fashion in estimating the worth of a scale. They have concentrated upon comparing the variation of responses to each item to the variance of each respondent's summed score. Therefore, unlike Guttman and Green's, analyses of this approach can be based upon either dichotomous or multi-level data.

The key to understanding this index is the following: the larger the value of the statistic, the better the reliability, because the program subtracts 1 from the ratio of item-total score variance. "When each person maintains the same relative position on every item and the total score, the value of the ratio becomes smaller,

6. *Ibid.*, p. 34.
7. *Ibid.*, p. 39.

approaching almost 0, and the overall value of the statistic becomes larger." [8]

Since K-R 20 does not consider the potential variance of each item, a corrected version of the K-R 20 was developed. It takes the maximum potential variance into consideration given the obtained distribution.

According to Burns, all the statistics discussed already are fundamental in testing the cohesiveness of the scale. "If the OBVERSE and REVERSE halves correlate significantly higher than zero, if the Kuder-Richardson reliabilities are significantly greater than zero, if each item correlates with the sum of the other items significantly greater than zero, there is significant cohesiveness among the items. Similarly, if we had applied a Goodman test to the Green B reproducibility and found it significant, then some significant degree of cohesiveness among the items would have been demonstrated." [9]

However, a scale could meet all the criteria of minimal cohesiveness but be a two-factored set of items. In other words, the scale could be measuring more than one single variable.

In order to test the single factoredness of the scale more precisely, the ATSCALE program used factor analysis. It used a modification of Thurstone's method designed to be optimal if single factoredness were actually the case.

The first estimate of the loading or correlation of each item with the common factor is a derivation of the corrected item—total correlation, the AGRAWAL COMMUNALITY ESTIMATE. It gives us some indication of how each item is related to the total score where the total score is taken to be the best estimate we have of the single trait or underlying factor that we are trying to measure.

The key to understanding the result of the single factor analysis is the Residual Matrix. The smaller the Residual Matrix the greater the probability that the questionnaires are indeed measuring a single trait or underlying dimension.

The last test for single factoredness is the Wollins Index of Single Factoredness. It is important because it approaches the ideal factoredness independent of the number of cases. A value of .75 may turn out to be the lower bounds of acceptable unidimensionality for this test.

---

8. *Ibid.*, p. 45.
9. *Ibid.*, p. 59.

PILOT STUDY RESULTS: RELIABILITY AND VALIDITY

In order to design the final version of the questionnaire, the following sections were evaluated through the ATSCALE program: Equity, Identification, Role Perception, Organizational Role Expectation, Academic Freedom, Trust, Warmth, and Participation in Decision Making. Some of the sections, such as Structure, Perception of Outsider Power, etc. were not included in this analysis because they were added after the pilot study.

The procedure used was to submit each section to the ATSCALE program and consider the index. The items with lower intercorrelation were omitted from the scale until we got an adequate item intercorrelation, good homogeneity and consistency index, and adequate results in the single factoredness analysis.

Another criterion that we used to determine which index could be included in the final questionnaire was its degree of predictive validity. If the behavior of the variable was consistent with the theory, and produced a significant correlation, we included the items in their final version.

The equity section originally was formed from nine items. After several analyses, we got a Kuder- Richardson index of .271. In addition the inferred average inter-item correlation was .271. This correlation is considered a moderate one, but we concluded that according to this index the equity section showed a sufficient degree of cohesiveness among items.

The Wollins index, which is one of the tests that the ATSCALE used to analyze single factoredness, was .9339. The probability (chance) of this section measuring more than one trait was low, and we decided to include it in the final questionnaire.

The last index considered in this analysis was the index which intended to measure the variable "trust". We got poor results, showing that the section was not tapping a single variable. The corrected Kuder-Richardson was .07. The inferred average inter-item correlation was −.073, and its Wollin Index of Single Factoredness was .3850. The sigma residual was a high .1362. Of course, these findings demonstrated that this scale was not unidimensional. A New scale was designed to replace the original scale.

Some of the scales do not appear in this analysis because they were either designed after the pilot study or are the product of a combination of several variables. For example, the "satisfaction"

4.

index, mean differences in role perception, and participation in decision making, were not submitted to the ATSCALE analysis.

Other variables such as organizational role expectation and role perception were submitted to the ATSCALE program in the analysis of the final questionnaire.

TEST OF RELIABILITY AND VALIDITY OF THE FINAL QUESTIONNAIRE

Although we used the ATSCALE program to design the final questionnaire, we used it again to asses the reliability and validity of the data collected in the final study. Before analyzing the data, we submitted each section of the questionnaire to the ATSCALE program in order to eliminate the items that seemed unscalable. Using this procedure we reduced the probability of measuring a multidimensional variable in the sections.

The section which measured "trust" was the first to be considered. The corrected Kuder-Richardson coefficient was improved. We got .410. However the inferred average inter-item correlation was still a low .105. But the sigma residual was very small, and the Wollins Index of Single Factoredness was quite high, .966. We decided that the scale could be included in the analysis of the final data with some assurance that it measured a unidimensional variable.

After several analyses, we threw out some of the items which were included in the scale on equity. The remaining items showed an acceptable degree of cohesiveness. The revised scale produced a Guttman coefficient of reproducibility of .94, and the coefficient of reproducibility of Green B was .96. Although the corrected Kuder Richardson index was only .312, we considered that the degree of cohesiveness shown by the scale was adequate. Its average inter-item correlation was .28. Since the sigma residuals obtained was low, .0406, and the Wollins Index of Single Factoredness was .864, we concluded that the scale presented an adequate degree of unidimensionality; therefore, we included this scale in the final analysis of the data.

The items thath we included in the final analysis in order to measure the variable "identification" produced the following results: corrected Kuder-Richardson .472, inferred average inter-item correlation 14; sigma residual .0505, and Wollins Index of Single Factoredness .876.

The section of "academic freedom" has less than four items; consequently, the ATSCALE did not test its degree of unidimensionality. However, the index which measured the degree of cohesiveness of the items produced a highly significant coefficient. The Guttman coefficient of reproducibility was .969, the Green B was also .969. The corrected Kuder-Richardson index was very high, .709, and the inferred average of inter-item correlation was .453.

According to the typical standard used to determine the degree of cohesiveness and unidimensionality of the scales, the coefficients must be highly significant over zero. Our section on Role Perception showed the following results: the corrected Kuder-Richardson index was .518, the average inter-item correlation was .19, and the Wollins Index Of Single Factoredness was .826. Although these are not strong results they are considered adequate enough to include the scale in the final analysis.

IV. PRESENTATION OF RESULTS

Having identified and operationalized the variables and described the statistical tests, our next step is to present and discuss the results. Each proposition will be discussed in light of the results, in their order of presentation.

I. THE ELABORATED PATH-GOAL MODEL

Our first set of propositions concerned the path-goal model prevalent in the literature. These propositions hypothesized a relationship between reward expectancies and effort; effort, role expectations and performance and between performance, equity and job satisfaction. There were also corollary propositions attempting to explain role perceptions. In general the propositions implicit in the path-goal model were only moderately successful in their correlations and significance.

A. The relationship between reward expectancies and effort

Hypothesis A-1 stated that the value of the reward and the probability that effort leads to reward should explain the professor's effort.

In order to test this hypothesis, a simple correlation between the combination of the value of the reward times the perceived effort-reward probability with effort was conducted.

We were also interested in how the value of reward and the perceived effort-reward probability *combined* to produce effort. Therefore an additive model and a multiplicative model were tested. Table 4-1 shows the results obtained.

Table 4-1

Correlation Analysis of the Additive and Multiplicative Model of Job Effort

Predictors	Dep. Variable	Coefficient	No. of Cases	Significance
IRW + EFF$_1$	EFF$_2$	.2133	193	.001
IRW + EFF$_1$	EFF$_2$	.2066	193	.001

where IRW represents the variable value of the reward, EEF$_1$ represents the perceived effort-reward probability, and Eff$_2$ represents the professor's evaluation of his effort exerted at the university.

According to these results, the value of the reward and the perceived effort-reward probability combine to produce effort; but the association, even though significant, is only moderate when the correlation analysis is used.

Neither the multiplicative model nor the additive proved to be the better predictor of the variable effort.

Porter and Lawler's findings were similar to ours. According to them, "the evidence from the present study points to a consistent, although moderate, relationship between the degree to which pay is seen as a satisfier and the motivation to perform a job effectively. Positive relationships were found in both samples and when both the self and superiors' evaluations were used."[1]

Similar results were obtained by Mitchell and Pollard. They found that the correlation between the self-effort rating and its predictors was .33 (p < .01; N = 54).[2] They concluded that the fact that the correlation coefficient was low demostrated that probably the job effort model should be modified in order to take into account other variables.

Lawler and Suttle's finding followed the same tendency as the results reported above. They concluded, "in neither sample are the correlations between the expectancy attitudes and effort high."[3] Like Mitchell and Pollard, Lawler and Suttle concluded that additional information is probably needed in order to increase the power of the expectancy measures to predict effort. According to their opinion, the measure of the degree of attractiveness of

1. Porter and Lawler, *op. cit.*, p. 90.
2. Mitchell and Pollard, *op. cit.*, p. 6.
3. Lawler and Suttle, *op. cit.*, p. 17.

various levels of performance is necessary in order to predict the amount of effort that the individual will exert on the job. "The model predicts that individuals will pick that level of performance which is most attractive. Thus, knowing how attractive good performance is to individuals gives some idea how likely they are to perform well because on the average people for whom it is very attractive should be better performers than people for whom it is less attractive."[4]

The model tested by Pritchard and Sanders predicted self-reported effort fairly well. "Taken as a whole, the data tended to offer some support for the basic expectancy-valence model, E (V * 1). The entire model correlated fairly high with self-reported effort, but relationships with supervisory ratings were low. The multiplicative relationship was found to predict no better than additive relationship between the variables.[5]

As we see, the model has been supported by some studies, but none of these studies found that the predictors were highly associated with the variable "effort." The researchers who conducted these studies presented several reasons to explain the findings. It seems that in order to improve the predictive power of the model, further investigation is needed to determine if other variables must be taken into account.

Nevertheless, some factors related to the methodology of the study and the research site may be considered in order to explain the results presented by our data.

The data showed that the variable "effort" did not have a significant amount of variability. On a scale of seven points, its mean was 6.04, and its standard deviation is 1.2. We assume that the statistics of the variabe "effort" demonstrate its lack of variability; therefore it is possible that the correlation obtained is a product of this limitation.

An explanation of the behavior of this variable could be put forth. It is possible that the professor tends to rank his effort on the job high because it is socially desirable. In other words, even though the questionnaires were anonymous, the tendency may have been to rank effort high because everybody would expect that a professor in the university would be dedicated (high effort means great dedication).

---

4. *Ibid.*, p. 18.
5. Robert Pritchard and M. Sanders, «The Influence of Valence, Instrumentality, and Expectancy on Effort and Performance,» *Journal of Applied Psychology*, 1973, 57, 55-60, pp. 58-59.

Another explanation would be that the professor believes that the quality of his performance is not associated with the amount of effort exerted at the university. "A clever professor doesn't have to put out a lot of effort in order to teach a good course." As a matter of fact, sometimes the word "effort" has the connotation that the person has to try hard because he does not have enough ability and knoweldge to perfom the job. If the professors understood the question which measured the variable "perceived effort-reward probability" in the way we mentioned above, it is possible that although they are actually exerting effort at the university, they did not answer the question in a proper way. Probably it would be useful in future research to use "dedication" instead of "effort."

Another explanation would be that the variable "perceived effort-reward probability" was related by the professor with the university rewards such as tenure, promotion, and other extrinsic rewards; therefore, because the professor would be motivated by the intrinsic to a greater extent than by the extrinsic reward, he would not consider that there is a high association between his effort and the possibility of attaining a reward.

Of course, the type of rewarding process used by the university could be an explanation of our findings. We discussed above that tenure, promotion, and fringe benefits are not contingent upon the professor's performance, which could possibly be the reason that the value of the reward times the perceived effort-reward probability explains only a moderate amount of the variability of the variable "effort."

In summary, the data showed statistically significant results when the job effort model was tested, although the variables were not highly correlated. The fact that the association between the predictors and effort was in the predicted direction show that the theory is not inadequate. Probably if we design better measures of the variable and if we conduct the test in a setting where extrinsic rewards are more thoroughly contingent upon the quality of the individual's performance, we will be able to find more significant results.

B. The relationship between effort, role perception and performance evaluation

Hypothesis A-2 was proposed in order to analyze the determinants of the chairman's evaluation of the quality of the performance produced by the professor. The Porter and Lawler model proposes that ability, role perception, and effort combine in order to produce performance. We consider that the degree of role accuracy is a significant determinant of the way the chairman ranks the quality of the performance produced by the professor. We propose that even though the professor sees the relation between rewards and performance, and has the ability necessary to do a good job and exert high effort to perform his job effectively, his performance is not going to be considered good by the chairman unless the chairman perceives that the professor is engaged in the appropriate activities.

Therefore we proposed hypothesis B-1, which said that the professor's performance is a function of effort times the degree of role agreement.

Of course, the measure of effort and performance used in this hypothesis was the chairman's rating because our objective was to analyze the determinants of the chairman's evaluation of the professor's performance. Also, in the Porter and Lawler model the variable "performance" is interpretable in two ways: as the perceptions of the organization regarding an individual's activity, and as the individual's perception of his activity.

This hypothesis was tested through product-moment correlation analysis. The following table show the results obtained.

Table 4-2

Correlation Analysis of the Relationship Between
Role Perceptions and Chairman's Evaluation
of the Professor's Performance

Dep. Variable	Ind. Variable	Coefficient	Significance	No. of Cases
PERFCH	$EFF_2 \times VAR201$	.1302	.059	145
PERFCH	$EFF_2 \times VAR202$	.2095	.008	134

These results do not necessarily support the hypotheses. We would expect to find a negative direction in the signs of the coefficient, if role discrepancy were a strong enough variable in the equation. It should be noted, for example, that where there is a relatively strong relationship (between PERFCH and EFF_2 X VAR202) the sign is perhaps positive because of the imbedded relationship between PERFCH and EFF_2 (.4232; sig = .000). In fact, the intercorrelations between performance and effort evaluations of professors and their chairmen is illuminating as to the complexity of the relationships involved:

Table 4-2-1

Intercorrelations between Performance and
Effort Evaluations

	PERF	PERFCH	EFF$_2$	EFFCH
PERF		—.0575	.0859[++]	.5347*
PERFCH			.4232*	.2945*
EFF$_2$				.1398[+]

* $p < .000$
[+] $p < .05$
[++] $p < .10$

First, it should be noted that there is little or no connection between how a professor rates his effort and how he rates his performance. On the other hand, there is a very strong relationship between how the professor rates his performance and how the chairman rates his effort (but not how he [the chairman] rates his performance). The idea of effort is clearly a factor in the situation. Furthermore, the chairman does not evaluate the professor's performance consistently with the professor's own evaluation of his performance. Nor are the professor's and the chairman's evaluation of the professor's efforts strongly related. It is almost as if the following inverse relationship obtained: what is meant by *performance* to the professor is understood as *effort* by the chairman (PERF highly correlating with EFFCH) and what is understood as *effort* by the professor is understood as performance by the chairman (EFF$_2$ highly correlating with PERFCH).

A second point about the relationships in Table 4-2 is that the professor's evaluation of effort and the chairman's evaluation of performance are strongly correlated in a positive direction, perhaps reducing the directional effects of role discrepancy. We do find that when we correlate PERF and EFF$_2$ X VAR 201 or VAR 202 that the weak positive relationship between PERF and EFF$_2$ does give a negative direction to the coefficients:

Table 4-2-2

Correlation Analysis of the Relationship Between
Role Perception and the Professor's Evaluation
of his Performance

Dep. Variable	Ind. Variable	Coefficient	Significance	No. of Cases
PERF	$EFF_2 \times$ VAR 201	—.4878	.000	178
PERF	$EFF_2 \times$ VAR 202	—.4264	.000	188

In general, the results do not support hypothesis A-2 except in the case of the self-rating measure of performance. Even if we substitute the chairman's evaluation of effort (EFFCH), for the chairman's evaluation of performance (PERFCH) the results are not consistently in the direction predicted.

Table 4-2-3

Correlation Analysis of Effort (Chairman's Rating)
with the Two Indexes of Role Disagreement

Dep. Variable	Ind. Variable	Coefficient	Significance	No. of Cases
EFFCH	Var. 202	—.2905	.000	158
EFFCH	Var. 201	.2544	.003	120

The differences in this case may lie with the meaning of variable 201 which is a reflection of the discrepancy of attitudes towards the *importance* of various activities and may not be reflected in the *actual* behavior of the professors, although it is difficult to understand why the discrepancy would be positively associated with the chairman's evaluation.

In effect, both indexes are measuring different attitudes and perceptions. Index 202 measured the difference in time allocation. We asked the chairman his opinion about how the professor should allocate his time, and compared it with the way that the professor said that he allocated his time at the university. This index measures the difference between what the chairman believes the professor should do and what the professor actually does.

On the other hand, index 201 is an attitudinal measure. It measures the opinion of the chairman and the professor about the importance of certain professorial activities such as work on committees, getting a Ph.D., improving the teaching methods for his courses, etc. We assume that index 202 is a better measure of role accuracy than index 201 because it measures the difference between what the professor is doing and what the chairman considers he should do. But index 201 measures attitudes and opinions that do not necessarily determine the professor's behavior. A professor could believe that work in committees is not important to the attainment of the university goals, but if the chairman asks him to work on a committee he would nevertheless probably comply with the chairman's recommendation. It is possible that the chairman and the professor may disagree on many aspects of role definition, and the chairman might never be aware of this disagreement. For example, it is possible that a professor considers that work on a committee is not the appropriate role of a professor, but since the chairman never asks him to work on a committee he doesn't perceive that the professor disagrees with him.

However, both indexes provide useful information. One provides attitudinal information and the other, perceptual information. Hence, we have to analyze the findings using different perspectives.

According to the findings provided through index 202, the greater the degree of role disagreement between the professor and the chairman, the lower the chairman ranks the amount of effort exerted by the professor.

These findings are consistent with Wall and Adams' conclusions.[6] They found that salesmen were ranked as high performers when their superiors perceived that they did what the superior suggested to them.

However, the results did not substantiate the proposition presented when index 201 was used in the analysis. It showed that the higher the role disagreement, the higher the chairman ranked the amount of effort exerted by the professors. This finding is difficult to explain. Our best guess is that even though the chairman has highly different opinions as to the value of various role activities, he ranks the professor high on effort since he assesses effort on the basis of daily activities. This may mean furthermore that the role activities in VAR 201 are in conflict with the role activities in 202. Although some of the activities in 201 are of a more episodic rather than a daily type it is not clear that they are in direct

---

6. Wall and Adams, *op. cit.*, p. 406.

conflict. More study would be needed to determine if this were so.

The findings, although not in the form initially expected, are of sufficient interest to ask (as in hypotheses A-3.1 and A-3.2) what the determinants of role discrepancy might be.

C. The relationship between rewards or social influence and role perceptions

The first of our hypotheses, hypothesis A-3.1 stated that the degree of role accuracy between professor and chairman is a function of the value of the reward times perceived effort-reward probability.

We assume that given that the professor believes that the chairman has significant influence over the university rewarding process, he will attempt to follow his role definition if the rewards are attractive and if he perceives that behaving in the way the chairman expects will lead to the attainment of the desired rewards.

A correlation anlysis between the combination of the value of reward times the perceived effort-reward probability and both indexes of role accuracy was conducted. The results obtained are presented in the Table 4-3.

Table 4-3-1

Correlation Analysis of Role Accuracy with the
Combination of Value of Reward Times the
Perceived Effort-Reward Probability

Predictors	Dep. Variable	Coeffi- cient	Signifi- cance	No. of Cases
IRW * EFF$_1$	Var. 202	.0566	.259	132
IRW * EFF$_1$	Var. 201	—.0276	.391	103

The results did not substantiate proposition A-3.1. According to the findings, the combination of the value of reward times the perceived effort-reward probability were associated with neither Var. 202, nor with variable 201.

These results demonstrated that the chairman's role definition is not considered significant by the professor in the determination of whether he deserves the university's rewards. Otherwise, the degree of role accuracy would be high, at least in the case of the professors who consider the university's rewards attractive. We assume that the number of professors who desire to attain promotion, tenure, and other university rewards must be significant, because many of the intrinsic rewards are contingent on the attainment of those extrinsic rewards mentioned. Let's consider for example, a professor who is highly motivated by the satisfaction of teaching. He enjoys the teaching activities and he is not concerned with salary, promotion, etc. He must get tenure in order to still have the satisfaction of teaching, because at the end of five years he could not continue teaching if he did not have a permanent position at the university. Therefore the intrinsic rewards is contingent on the extrinsic reward.

Another interpretation would be that the professor perceives that he will get the university's rewards even though his role perception disagrees with that of the chairman. It is possible that the professor considers that in the university there are many ways to perform good work and he will not be penalized because he does not define his job in the same way as the chairman.

It is also possible that the chairman's evaluation does not affect the probability that the professor attains the rewards offered by the university. As we discussed already, it is difficult for the professor to consider the chairman's evaluation fundamental in the rewarding process if the university maintains the practice of rewarding professors to stimulate them toward the desired performance without the establishment of a contingency relationship between effective performance and the subsequent attainment of the university's rewards.

Even though role accuracy affects the way the chairman ranks the professor's effort, as Table 4-3 shows, the value of reward times the perceived effort-reward probability does not affect role accuracy. Because the professor does not consider the chairman's evaluation as determinant of the rewards, he therefore does not have to take into account the chairman's opinion of how he should define his job.

We believe that in the research setting where the supervisor has strong power in the rewarding process, the value of rewards times the perceived-effort probability is associated with the degree of role accuracy because the subordinate knows that his supervisor's opinion is a relevant determinant of the organizational reward; therefore, his expectation to attain a reward may be based on his perception that he is doing what his supervisor considers he should do (role accuracy).

Hypothesis A-3.2 is closely related to the proposition discussed above. The function of this proposition is to explain how the degree of role accuracy between the professor and the chairman is developed. It attempts to test whether the degree of role accuracy is a function of the power that the persons or group that constitute the professor's work environment have to influence the professor's behavior. It states that the greater the relevance the professor ascribes to the chairman's opinion about the way to define the professor's roles, and the more often he interacts with the chairman, the greater should be the professor's agreement with the chairman's definition of the role of the professor at the university.

We assumed that the chairman was the person in the professor's job environment who exerts the highest degree of influence over his behavior.

In order to test this hypothesis, a Pearson correlation was run between the importance that the professor ascribes to the chairmans' opinion about the way he is performing his job times the frequency with which he gets information about the chairman's opinion and the role accuracy indexes (Var. 201, Var. 202). The same statistical test was conducted with the rest of the persons or groups that we considered as possible sources of influence on the professor's behavior in his job environment.

Table 4-3-2

Pearson Correlation of Var. 201 and 202 with
PAXDA, PAXDB, PAXDC, PAXDD, PAXDE, PAXDF, PAXDG, AND TOSI

Variable	Variable	Coefficient	Significance	No. of Cases
Var. 202	PAXDA	.1315	.031	203
Var. 201	PAXDA	.0827	.145	166
Var. 202	PAXDB	.3780	.000	203
Var. 201	PAXDB	.0443	.286	165
Var. 202	PAXDC	.2533	.000	203
Var. 201	PAXDC	—.0674	.196	163
Var. 202	PAXDD	.4211	.000	197
Var. 201	PAXDD	—.0896	.129	162
Var. 202	PAXDE	.7143	.000	203
Var. 201	PAXDE	—.1045	.104	161
Var. 202	PAXDF	.6913	.000	203
Var. 201	PAXDF	—.0649	.207	160
Var. 202	PAXDG	.6871	.000	203
Var. 201	PAXDG	.0293	.356	161
Var. 202	TOSI	.6192	.000	197
Var. 201	TOSI	—.0819	.152	159

where: Var. 202 and Var. 201 represent the disagreement between the professor's role perception and organizational role expectation; PAXDA represents the importance of the opinion of students who take classes with the professor times the frequency with which the professor hears about their opinion; PAXDB represents the relevance of the opinion of the student in general times the frequency with which the professor hears about it; PAXDC represents the importance of the chairman's opinion to the professor times the frequency with which he hears about it; PAXDD represents the relevance of the dean's opinion to the professor times the frequency with which the professor hears about it; PAXDE represents the importance that a professor ascribes to the opinion of colleagues in other universities times the frequency with which he hears about it; PAXDF represents the relevance that the professor ascribes to the opinion of his colleagues in his department times the frequency with which he hears about it; PAXDG represents the importance that a professor ascribes to the opinion of the people outside of his university times the frequency with which he hears about it; and TOSI represents all the sources of influence together.

The result does not substantiate our hypothesis. We found a significant positive correlation between Var. 202 and PAXDC: .2533 at the .000 level of significance. (The correlation with Var .201 was here and in the other cases non-significant.) It means that even if the opinion of the chairman is important to the professors, it does not produce an agreement in the way both define the roles of the professors. We hypothesized that the greater the importance that the professor ascribes to the opinion of the chairman about the way he is performing, the greater the congruity between their opinions (opinion of the chairman and opinion of the professor about what should be the proper role of the professor). We considered that given that the chairman seems to be the person in the professor's job environment with the most power to coerce or reward the professor, his (chairman's) opinion must be the most relevant to the professor; therefore, the professor would try to define his role in a way similar to that in which the chairman defined it. However, the results demonstrated that the importance that the professor gives to the chairman's opinion times the frequency that he hears about it does not produce role agreement; but even more important, they demonstrated that to a greater or lesser extent, the opinions of the rest of the persons in the job environment are strongly associated with the discrepancy between the professor's and chairman's definitions of the role of the professor.

As a matter of fact, according to the differences obtained in the correlations, the chairman is the second-least influencer among all the persons or groups of persons which have influence over the professor's behavior. The students who take courses with the professor are the source of influence with the least power among all the sources of influence.

Even though the chairman and the students who attend the professor's courses are very often in contact with him, they do not have much influence upon the professor's behavior. These findings do not support the proposition that the chairman and the students have great influence over the professor's behavior. It seems that neither the chairman nor the students have enough power to influence the rewarding process and consequently to influence the professor's behavior. In effect, the discrepancy between the professor's and his chairman's role perceptions are much more strongly related to the influences of colleages and people outside the university than to either students or to the chairmen themselves. The relatively low correlation between chairman influence and discrepent role perceptions may be related to DeVries' findings that the expectations of the organizational superiors do not influence directly the behavior of their subordinates. Just as in our finding, he found that the chairman's expectations do not determine the way in which the professor defines his roles. His explanation is that it is possible that the departmental executive, because of idiosyncratic role expectations, has become a marginal member of his professional community. DeVries said that "not only does the executive office frequently have little formal authority over his faculty, but in addition, by the nature of the role allocations required of him he may lose whatever informal influence he had originally with his colleagues." [7]

The fact that colleagues in other universities and people outside the university have high influence upon the professor's behavior demonstrated a high interaction of the professor with the elements in the external environment of the university. This may be explained by the following reason. First, it is possible that the professor is greatly concerned with society: therefore, he perceives that the university must respond to some extent to the opinion of the people in the community. Another explanation could be that the university is higly influenced by politicians, and since they have strong power over the university's decisions, the pro-

7. David L. DeVries, *op. cit.*, p. 23.

fessors are very concerned with their opinion. Also, the professor is higly self-esteem oriented and therefore is used to paying attention to colleagues and to people outside the university in order to get feedback about his reputation. It is also possible that the professor is really concerned about his image outside the university because it may affect the possibility of his finding consulting positions or appointments to important positions outside the university.

The fact that professors pay attention to colleagues in other universities is encouraging because it means that they interact with them, and this contributes to the diffusion of knowledge and the integration of the professionals.

Another important fact that we want to point out is the high association between PAXDF and Var. 202. This means that the colleagues in the department are a great source of influence on the professor's behavior.

This finding is consistent with the theory propounded by Parsons [8] and Caplow and McGee,[9] among others. According to them, departmental colleagues are important forces of control over faculty members. They are a sample of professional colleagues and the professor may receive from them the expectation that other professionals have about the roles. In addition, the departmental colleagues participate in many decisions that concern the professor such as decisions of whether or not the professor deserves tenure or deserves a promotion, recommendations to appoint the head of the department, and so forth. Therefore, the departmental colleagues have enough power to exert influence over the professor's behavior.

As we said before, we don't consider that the chairman has no influence over faculty behavior. Rather, we maintain that his influence is not strong enough to determine the way the professor defines his role. Again we emphasize the importance of the reward and coercive power.

If the chairman were to have enough power to determine whether the professor deserves a reward or not, he might have stronger influence over his behavior than in the present position. In other words, we postulated that the behavior could not be controlled if the person who attempts to do it does not have enough power to influence the subordinate's behavior.

8. Talcott, Parsons, «Suggestions for a Sociological Approach to the Theory of Organizations, II,» *Administrative Science Quarterly*, 1956, *1*, pp. 225-239.
    9. Caplow and McGee, *op. cit.*

The fact that the opinions of all the persons or groups of persons in the professor's job environment were not associated with the index of role accuracy constituted by Var. 201 means that the opinion of the professor about what activities are relevant in order for the university goals to be attained are not influenced by any one of those sources of influence. The concept of "university goals" is very broad and it is possible that it is inadequate to tap role perception.

D. The relationships between performance, perceived equity, role perceptions and satisfaction

The next set of hypotheses are related to the degree of satisfaction experienced by the professor. According to the model of Porter and Lawler, satisfaction is a function of rewards which are in turn a function of performance. They assume that the individual gets the reward after producing a performance that the organization considers meaningful and therefore rewards in order to reinforce the individual's behavior. Of course, this model assumes that in the organization the rewards are determined by the individual's performance. In addition, the model proposes that the individual must perceive that the reward obtained is equitable, otherwise he is not going to experience satisfaction with the rewards.

Following this line of thought, we proposed hypothesis A-4-1. It stated that the satisfaction experienced by the professor in the university is the function of his performance, when he perceives that the rewards obtained are equitable. We operationalized satisfaction in two ways. First, we determined the difference between the professor's indicator of the current level of rewards they experience (PREW) and the level of rewards they expressed as ought to be present. This variable (LSAT) we took as lack of satisfaction. Secondly, we had the professors indicate on a seven point scale their general level of satisfaction (GSAT). These two variables correlated in the expected direction, ($-.2286$; sig. .078) but the relationship was not a strong one.

The results (see Table 4-4-1) show that equity is a significant factor in the professor's feelings of satisfaction. Furthermore, as the perception of equity increases, the perception as to the level of rewards currently available to the job increases (PREW).

There is also a correlation (.3810; sig. .001) between general satisfaction and the perception of current reward levels (PREW). But while the chairman's evaluation of the professor's performance relates quite strongly to the professor's feelings of general satisfaction (.4817; sig. .001) the chairman's evaluation does not relate to the current level of rewards as perceived by the professors, nor does the chairman's evaluation relate to the lack of satisfaction with rewards (LSAT).

Table 4-4-1

The Relationships Between Rewards, Satisfaction and Equity

	EQ	GSAT	LSAT	PERF	PERFCH	PREW
EQ		.2723++	—.3867++	.0540	.0225	.3810*
GSAT			—.2286*	.0543	.4817*	.4210*
LSAT				.1469	—.0058	.2830+
PERF					—.0750	.1940+
PERFCH						.0285

$* \ p < .001$
$++ \ p < .005$
$+ \ p < .01$
$* \ p < .10$

These results seem to indicate that the chairman does not play a significant role in the direct rewarding process. His evaluation is not related to the degree of satisfaction with rewards as experienced by the professor.

This weak relationship between the degree of reward satisfaction experienced by the professor and the chairman's evaluation may be because it seems that most of the professor's sources of satisfaction are intrinsic, and these types of rewards are not mediated by the university. In other words, it is possible that these results are due to the fact that the professor feels much satisfaction when he attains an intrinsic reward.

Another explanation of the lack of association found between the reward satisfaction experienced by the professor and the chairman's evaluation of performance would be that the rewards in the university are not contingent upon the professor's performance. If the rewarding process is not based on the professor's performance we could not expect any association between satisfaction and performance. The theory is straightforward: performance and satisfaction are associated only when the organizational rewards are a function of the individual's performance.

This explanation has support in past studies. Porter and Lawler found that the perception of fulfillment was related to performance when actual extrinsic rewards were given more or less in proportion to actual differences in performance.[10]

Graen concluded that changes in effort and satisfaction respectively are the consequences of being rewarded contingent upon effective performance by an organization that maintains a reciprocating climate.[11]

Deci concluded that money would not motivate the individual to work, unless the performance was perceived as instrumental to receiving the money.[12]

Greene found that merit pay was the function of the degree of satisfaction experienced by the individual in the organization.[13]

As those studies concluded, if the rewards are not contingent upon the individual's performance, performance could not lead to reward satisfaction. On the other hand there is a strong relationship between the chairman's evaluation and the general feeling of satisfaction felt by the professor. This may mean that the attitude of the chairman towards the professor does affect the professor's feeling of satisfaction.

Hypothesis A-4.2 assumes that the degree of role accuracy is associated with the degree of satisfaction experienced by the professor. We based this proposition on the findings of researchers such as Kahn et al.,[14] Greene and Organ,[15] Lyons,[16] Rizzo et al.,[17] who reported that the degree of satisfaction experienced by the individual in the organization was associated with role accuracy, role consensus, and role clarity.

If the rewards are contingent upon the individual's performance, and if the individual's performance (chairman's rating) is a function of role accuracy, it is logical that the satisfaction experienced by the individual in the organization be associated with the degree of role accuracy between the chairman and professor.

---

10. Porter and Lawler, op. cit., p. 162.
11. George B. Graen, op. cit., p. 24.
12. Edward Deci, «The Effects of Contingent and Non-contingent Rewards and Controls of Intrinsic Motivation,» Organizational Behavior and Human Performance, 1972, 8, pp. 217-229.
13. Charles N. Greene, «Causal Connections Among Managers' Merit Pay, Job Satisfaction, and Performance,» Journal of Applied Psychology, 1973, 58, 95-100, p. 99.
14. Kahn et al., op. cit.
15. Greene and Organ, op. cit.
16. Lyons, op. cit.
17. Rizzo et al., op. cit.

In other words, if the chairman's evaluation determines whether the professor deserves a reward, and if this evaluation is a function of the degree of role accuracy, the professor who obtains a reward would have to comply with the chairman's role expectation.

The following table shows the results obtained when hypothesis A-4.2 was tested.

Table 4-4-2

Pearson's Correlation Between Reward Satisfaction
(Computed here as Lack of Satisfaction)
and VAR 202 and VAR 201

Ind. Variable	Dep. Variable	Coefficient	Significance	No. of Cases
VAR 202	LSATON	.1213	.168	65
VAR 201	LSATON	.0660	.170	83

Again, the results show that in the university the rewards are not contingent upon the professor's performance. The results show that role disagreement was not associated with the degree of dissatisfaction experienced by the professor. In other words, the professor does not try to comply with the chairman's role expectation because his rewards are not determined by the chairman's evaluation.

It is interesting that the fact that the chairman does not play a significant role in the rewarding process explains why role disagreement, even though it affects the way he ranks the professor's performance and effort, does not affect the professor's degree of satisfaction.

It should also be noted that there was no evidence that role discrepancies had any adverse effect on job satisfaction, at least as reported by the professors. VAR 201 negatively correlated with general satisfaction ($-.049$) and VAR 202 also negatively correlated with general satisfaction ($-.044$) but neither relationship was statistically significant.

II. ORGANIZATIONAL SETTING HYPOTHESES

The objective of this section is to report the findings of the hypotheses relating to the organizational setting. We will test the general proposition that these variables that constitute the organizational setting could affect to some extent the outcome proposed by the Porter and Lawler model of motivation.

A. The relationship between organizational setting and importance of rewards

It was hypothesized that the importance of the rewards available to the professor will be affected by various climate variables, especially academic freedom, trust, equity, identification, and warmth. Only academic freedom and identification showed a significant relationship to the professors' perceptions of rewards.

Table 4-5-1

The Relationship Between Organizational Setting
and Importance of Rewards

	Importance of Rewards
Academic Freedom	.103**
Trust	—.036
Equity	.086
Identification	.342*
Warmth	.036
Red Tape	—.208*

*p. < .01
**p. < .10

Furthermore, we might have expected the signs to show, in the opposite direction. That is, as climate is more satisfactory, there is less perceived importance for other and more performance-related types of rewards. But this was not the case.

We did find a negative correlation between red tape and the importance of job related rewards. This might be explained as follows. As red tape increases, perceived instrumentality and hence the values placed on job related rewards should decrease. As we shall see in the next section, we did find a negative relationship between red tape and perceived instrumentality.

B. The relationship between organizational setting and perceived effort-reward probability

We hypothesized that the professor's perception of instrumentality in obtaining job related rewards would be affected by academic freedom (this would affect his sense of being able to get intrinsic satisfaction from his effort), participation in decision-making, outsiders' influence on decision-making (and hence determining his performance requirements) and trust.

We found (Table 4-4-4), that all these variables did in fact correlate significantly (at the .01 level) with instrumentality. We found, furthermore, that other climate variables related to instrumentality as well. Red tape negatively correlated as might be expected. Structuring of activities (perhaps giving a necessary sense of order) correlated positively. Warmth, equity and identification showed a strong relationship. While a supportive climate (warmth) might be seen as a cause of instrumentality, it seems likely that identification is a consequence rather than a reason for perceived instrumentality. With our design, however, there was no way to test these relationships to determine the direction of their impact.

Table 4-5-2

The Relationship Between Organizational Setting and Perceived Effort-Reward Probability

	Perceived Effort-Reward Probability
Academic Freedom	.277*
Participation in decision-making	.134*
Outsider Influence	—.076
Trust	.349*
Red tape	—.264*
Warmth	.365*
Equity	.373*
Identification	.473*
Guidelines and procedures	.107*

*p. < .01

C. The relationship between organizational setting, performance and job satisfaction

The two principal outcomes of the Porter and Lawler model are the individual's effort and performance. The satisfaction experienced by the individual will be a function of the rewards intrinsic and extrinsically related to this performance.

However, many studies have concluded that these outcomes of the Porter and Lawler model would be a function of other variables not included in the path-goal model.

For example, Patchen, in his research among TVA employees, found that the feeling of identification of the employees with the organization induced them to increase their production.[18] It seems that when the individual perceives that he is getting that desired reward from the organization it would induce him to support the organization in order to continue getting the rewards.

Litwin and Stringer, in their literature review, found that the feeling of identification increases not only the individual's performance, but also the interpersonal sensitivity and interpersonal trust.[19] We did, in fact, find a strong relationship between identification and trust (.554 at the .01 level of significance).

The fact that the feeling of identification will increase interpersonal trust is quite important in the university setting, because a great deal of the professor's work requires the cooperation of his colleagues. Therefore, if the feeling of identification will increase interpersonal trust, interpersonal comunication will increase also.

Hall *et al.* found that the feeling of identification results in intrinsic need satisfaction.[20]

In summary, it seems that many studies have found that the feeling of identification increases the individual's performance and his satisfaction, and leads him to develop a positive attitude toward the organization.

We hypothesized that if the feeling of identification leads people to defend and support the organization, it would affect to some extent the amount of effort exerted by them in the organization. The individual would know that in order for the organization to continue providing him with rewards and the means of satisfac-

---

18. Martin Patchen, *op. cit.*, p. 241.
19. Litwin and Stringer, *op. cit.*, p. 60.
20. D. Hall *et al.*, «Personal Factors in Organizational Identification,» *Administrative Science Quarterly*, 1970, 15, pp. 176-190.

tion, the organization must keep functioning. He also knows that his performance is fundamental in order to provide the profits or input that the organization needs to continue to function. Therefore, we propose that the amount of effort exerted by the individual would be a function of his perception that the organization which provides him with the desired rewards needs his performance in order to function.

Table 4-5-3 indicates that identification does correlate with general job satisfaction as do a number of climate variables (outsider influence, red tape, guidelines and procedures, trust, warmth, equity, identification.) These relationships were not quite as strong as the relationship specified in the path-goal model where we found general job satisfaction strongly correlated with chairman's evaluation of performance (.4817).

Table 4-5-3

The Relationship Between Organizational
Setting and Job Satisfaction

	Job Satisfaction	Lack of Reward Satis.
Academic Freedom	.071	—.305*
Participation in decision making	—.071	—.294*
Outsider influence	—.273*	.064
Red tape	—.124*	.060
Guidelines and procedures	.288*	—.298*
Trust	.346*	—.322*
Warmth	.151*	—.414*
Equity	.272*	—.388*
Identification	.289*	—.459*

*p. < .01

On the other hand, the chairman's evaluation of performance did not significantly (and negatively) correlate with lack of reward satisfaction as would have been expected. This failure of the model has been explained above. It is interesting to note that the climate variables do strongly correlate with a sense of reward deficiency. Here, in fact, we have a more persistent and stronger pattern of relationships. However, the direction of influence between the variables still remains in question as before because of our design.

With respect to effort and performance evaluations the evidence is much less definite. Trust was most persistently related to the evaluations (see Table 4-5-4). Because, however, of the

Table 4-5-4

The Relationship Between Organizational Setting and Effort and Performance Evaluations

	EFF₂	EFFEC	PERF	PERFCH
Red Tape	—.036	.210*	.091	.007
Guidelines and Procedures	.107*	—.095	—.375*	.373*
Academic Freedom	—.096***	—.142***	.066	—.088
Participation in Decision-Making	—.237*	—.053	—.058	—.018
Outsider Influence	—.130*	—.192*	—.088	—.257*
Trust	.076***	—.175*	—.468*	.358*
Warmth	—.190*	—.217*	—.079	—.149**
Equity	.013	.054	.054	.023
Identification	.041	—.287	—.287*	.144*

*p. < .01
**p. < .05
***p. < .10

problems involved in the meanings of these evaluations it is difficult to interpret the data. The directions of the signs are not always as we had expected. We expected that climate variables would positively correlate with evaluations.

However, self-evaluation either did not significantly correlate with climate variables and when it did correlate significantly the signs were in the wrong direction in the case of academic freedom, participation in decision making and warmth. Self-evaluation of performance correlated more strongly with climate variables, especially in the case of trust and guidelines and procedures. Again, however, trust and identification negatively correlated with performance evaluations made by the professors when we would have expected them to correlate positively.

The chairman's evaluation of a professor's effort and performance also irregularly related to climate variables and again the direction of the signs were often unexpected. Red tape should have negatively correlated with evaluations. We had expected that academic freedom, participation in decision-making, trust, warmth, equity and identification would positively correlate with the evaluations. The chairman's evaluation of effort, however, negatively related to all of these except equity.

In the case of the chairman's evaluation of performance, guidelines and procedures, outsider influence, trust and identification did relate in the expected direction, but warmth did not.

The reasons for these mixed findings may lie in the instrument used to determine effort and performance evaluations, especially the question raised earlier as to what these mean to the participants in the study. A more interesting point may be, however, that climate has a complex relationship to job perceptions and this complex relationship needs to be sorted out by a more sophisticated methodology than that used in our study.

V. GENERAL CONCLUSIONS

The present study was undertaken for the purpose of evaluating a motivational model which seems useful to predict and explain the work behavior of the professor at the university. The test of the model focuses, especially, on role perception and on the effects that organizational setting have on variables of the model. In light of the results of the study one can assess the implications and speculate on directions for future research.

SUMMARY

One of the main outcomes of the motivational model presented in this study is the individual's effort. The model states that the value of the reward and the perceived effort-reward probability combine to produce effort. The multiplicative and the additive model were tested. Both performed nearly the same in predicting effort, although the multiplicative model was slightly stronger.

We concluded that these results supported the job effort model, but its predictive power was very low. Some reasons could be used to explain the results obtained. First, the results could be explained by methodological deficiencies. The data showed that the variable "effort" did not show a significant amount of variability. Therefore, it is possible that the coefficients obtained were the product of this limitation. An explanation of the lack of variability of the variable "effort" could be found in the deficiencies of the method used to measure it. Many researchers have reported the same phenomenon. Second, the concept of effort could be associated by the professor with the lack of ability, knowledge or capability to perform his job effectively and therefore they could not rank their effort low. Also, the data indicated that the meaning of effort and performance are more complex than was expected. Third, the type of rewarding process used by the universities in Puerto Rico appears not to be contingent upon the professor's performance. If the research site does not fulfill this condition, it is almost impossible for the model to work out well, because the model is based on the assumption that the individual must see his performance as instrumental in attaining the reward in order to exert effort.

Another hypothesis tested in this study was that the greater the amount of effort exerted by the professor, the higher will be his performance—assuming that he has an accurate role perception.

The findings did not strongly support this proposition when we used the chairman's evaluation of the professor's performance. The fact that there was a high degree of role accuracy between the professor and the chairman does not improve the correlation between the amount of effort exerted by the professor and his performance.

This result is consistent with the findings reported when the job effort model was tested. It seems that the professor does not think that he has to exert a great amount of effort in order to produce a relevant performance.

However, we have to repeat that this result could be explained by the lack of variability of the variable "effort."

The self performance model was not supported by the data, either. When effort (self-rating) times the value of reward was correlated with performance (self-rating), the correlation was very low ($.144$ $p < .035$; $N = 197$). The additive model produced non-significant results. On the other hand, there was a strong and significant correlation between the professor's own evaluation of his performance, his effort, and the discrepancy of roles. This is not produced by the potential tautology between the two self-evaluations since these of themselves did not correlate below the $.05$ level of significance.

Porter and Lawler's model also proposed to explain the degree of satisfaction experienced by the individual in the organization. The model predicts that the individual would experience satisfaction if his performance were rewarded with the rewards that he considered equitable.

The results did not support this proposition either. We found no significant association between the degree of satisfaction experienced by the individual and his performance (chairman rating), considering the variable "perceived equitable rewards" as the intervening variable. On the other hand, the chairman's evaluation correlated positively with general job satisfaction but not, as would have been expected, with level of satisfaction with rewards.

We concluded that these findings were consistent with the results obtained when the rest of the model was tested. If the professors does not perceive that the rewards attained in the organization are products of his performance, we would not expect any association between performance and the degree of reward satisfaction experienced by him in the university.

A secondary objective of this study was to analyze the function that role perception and role theory play in the interaction of the model's variables. Even though Porter and Lawler proposed in their model that the appropriateness of role perception is fundamental to producing meaningful performance, they never designed a job substantive method to measure the degree of role accuracy between the superior and subordinate.

Two indices of role accuracy were developed in this study. They were used to test the job performance model (chairman's rating) and the interrelation of role perception with other variables in the model.

The most salient finding obtained was that the chairman's rating of the professor's performance times the degree of role accuracy explains significantly the chairman's evaluation of the professor's performance. Another interesting finding was that the chairman's evaluation of the professor's effort is a function of role accuracy. In other words, when the professor defines his job in the same way as the chairman, the chairman ranks the amount of effort exerted by the professor at the university higher than when he doesn't.

The hypothesis that the chairman is the person in the professor's work environment with the strongest influence on the professor's behavior was tested. Following Raven's [1] theory of social influence, we assumed that the chairman would have the unique combination of reward, coercive and expertise power.

The procedure used to test this proposition was based upon Stinchombe's theory of the structure of attention which says that the effect of someone else's activity on the actions and attitudes of a person is a function of the probability that this person will pay attention to it, multiplied by the duration that the person's attention is focused on it.[2]

We found that the chairman is not the person in the profes-

1. B. H. Raven, *op. cit.*, pp. 371-382.
2. Arthur L. Stinchcombe, *op. cit.*, p. 236.

sor's work environment with the strongest power over the professor's behavior. As a matter of fact, the professor's colleagues in the department, colleagues in other universities, and people outside the university were identified by the professors as the greatest source of influence upon the professor's behavior. This, in effect, gave a very strong and positive relationship between these influences and role discrepancy.

Another purpose of this study was to analyze the impact of organizational variables upon the Porter and Lawler model. The basic assumption was that the organizational variables could affect the variables of the model and thereby affect the model's outcome: the prediction of the individual's effort, performance, and the degree of satisfaction experienced in the organization. We proposed that the organizational variables could be alternative explanations of the outcomes predicted and explained by the Porter and Lawler model.

We found that organizational variables do affect individual variables in the model of Porter and Lawler presented in this study. For example, the results showed that the value that a professor ascribes to a reward is associated in a negative way with the perception that there is red tape at the university. In other words, the greater the perception of red tape the lower the value of the reward.

We also found a higher correlation between the perceived effort-reward probability and "trust." The greater the professor's feeling of trust in the university, the greater his perception that his performance is instrumental in getting the desired reward.

These findings show that the value of the reward and the individual's perception of instrumentality are affected by organizational variables such as red tape, and others.

In general we found organizational setting variables to be successfully correlated to both general job satisfaction and to lack of satisfaction with rewards. These variables did better than the Porter and Lawler hypothesized relationship between performance evaluation and rewards (for reasons explained above), but not significantly better than a hypothesized relationship between performance evaluation and general job satisfaction.

The setting variables were least consistently successful in predicting effort and performance. Some variables, guidelines and trust, did as well as the Porter and Lawler model; other variables were counter-indicative to our expectations with respect to self-evaluations and chairman's evaluation of effort.

SOME IMPLICATIONS OF THE STUDY

The Porter and Lawler model explained little of the variance of the professor's performance and effort. The model did not explain the degree of reward satisfaction experienced by the professor in the university. We conclude that the reason for these results is that the rewarding process used by the university does not associate the university's reward with the professor's performance.

We based the conclusion presented above on the fact that the Porter and Lawler model required that the individual see his performance as an instrument to obtain rewards. If the individual does not see the rewards contingent on his performance he will not exert any effort to produce a significant performance. In addition, the reward satisfactions experienced by the individual in the organization can't be explained through the Porter and Lawler model if the individual's rewards are not tied to his performance. The individual performance and the degree of satisfaction experienced in the organization are associated only when the individual sees that his performance is an instrument to get the rewards that make the individual satisfied.

Therefore, if Puerto Rican universities continue with the present rewarding structure, Porter and Lawler's model is not going to be a useful approach to improving performance.

It seems, however, that the university does not have a clear means of controlling the professor's behavior through other influence strategies as well as through the rewarding process. For example, the results of this study showed that the chairman is not a strong influencer of professor's behavior. It is not possible to motivate the professor if the university does not have any method of reinforcing his positive behavior. If the university rewards the professor on a group basis, it is not able to affect the individual performance of its professors. Therefore, the university must rely on the power of the group of professors to affect the individual performance, but if the standards of performance of the professors are low, the quality of the university performance must be low and administration, including departmental structure, does not seem to be a strong enough factor for change.

Role theory seems to be useful in explaining a great deal of behavior in the university. For example, we found that the chairman tends to give a lower evaluation of the professor's effort when the latter disagrees with the way the chairman defines the

5.

professor's roles. On the other hand, role discrepancy did not seem to negatively affect performance evaluations.

Even though the chairman does not seem to have power over the professor's behavior, the fact that agreement in role definition improves the professor's evaluation of effort by the chairman is quite relevant. It indicates that the conflict that usually exists between the faculty and the administration is probably due in part to the lack of role agreement. Therefore, if the university wants to avoid this conflict it must realize the need to improve the degree of role accuracy between the professors and the administration.

THE RELEVANCE OF THESE FINDINGS TO THE ADMINIS-
TRATION OF THE UNIVERSITIES

These findings show the necessity to tie the university's rewards to the professor's performance. The university must have an instrument that permits it to influence the professor's work behavior.

The university must tie the professor's tenure and promotions to the quality of his performance. In order to do that the university must develop better instruments to evaluate the professor's performance.

More sources of satisfaction of intrinsic needs must be developed in the university. The university must provide some instruments to reward all the professors who make exceptional contributions to the university. In that way the professor can be motivated to do research, publish, and be involved in the solution of social problems.

Role agreement with intra-organizational others (as opposed to extra-organizational others) seems to be fundamental in order to improve the quality of the professor's performance. In addition, role accuracy is relevant in order to avoid conflict between the faculty and the administration. Therefore, we consider that the university must improve communications between its students, professors and administrators in order to define the institutional roles and improve the degree of role agreement between these three groups.

Finally, we consider that the administration of the university must realize the relevance of the organizational climate in order to explain the behavior of the individuals who work in the organization. The fact that some variables in the organizational setting seemed to affect the professor's expectation and perception demonstrate their relevance. The university must develop and adequate environment to stimulate the professor to innovate and use the maximum of his capabilities in his work.

THE NEED FOR IMPROVEMENT OF THE MEASUREMENT OF PATH-GOAL AND SETTING VARIABLES

Another problem demonstrated by the study was the necessity to determine the degree of contribution of each variable in the combination to produce effort and performance. Also the direction of influence among the variables. We consider this information critical if we want to determine the relevance of the variables. For example, which contributes more to explaining the amount of effort exerted by the individual at the organization: the value of reward or the perceived effort-reward probability? To what degree would the amount of effort be affected if the valence of reward decreases or if the perceived effort-reward probability decreases? To what extent must the valence of reward be affected in order that the individual decides not to exert effort? Which variable is more relevant to explain the individual's performance? It would especially be important for administrations to know whether perception of climate and feelings towards climate is affected by the level of reward satisfaction or vice-versa.

Our literature review shows that usually the lack of significant association has been explained by deficiencies in the measurement of the variables. Our study showed the same phenomenon. It seems that if we want to test the model with much more credence, we must improve the measurement of the model's variables, including more controlled circumstances in the design of our studies.

Finally, we want to add that the fact that since there has not been much research done in the area of organizational behavior in the university, research in this setting is quite relevant. The university plays a fundamental role in society; therefore, we have to improve our understanding of its operation in order to improve its effectiveness.

Finally, role theory seems to be useful to provide some understanding of the professor's behavior in the university. Even though we did some analysis of the determinants of role accuracy and the responsiveness of the professor to individuals or groups in his work environment, further research is needed. We consider that it is fundamental to determine which are the factors that lead the professor to respond to any source of influence.

5.*

Questionnaire

Section I

Below, are listed a number of things that you can either do in your job or can receive from your job. For each such thing, you will be asked to give four ratings: (a) How much is there now? (b) How much would you like it to be? (c) How much do you consider that your personal effort can affect the amount that you will get in the future? (d) How important is this to you?

Each rating will be a seven-point scale, which will look like this: (Minimum) 1 2 3 4 5 6 7 (Maximum).

1 — Possibilities of personal growth and development.

    a) How much is there now?   (Min) 1 2 3 4 5 6 7 (Max)

    b) How much would you like it to be?   (Min) 1 2 3 4 5 6 7 (Max)

    c) How much do you consider that your personal effort can affect the amount that you will get in the future?   (Min) 1 2 3 4 5 6 7 (Max)

    d) How important is this to you?   (Min) 1 2 3 4 5 6 7 (Max)

2 — The feeling that your job is highly respected in your community and country.

    a) How much is there now?   (Min) 1 2 3 4 5 6 7 (Max)

    b) How much would you like it to be?   (Min) 1 2 3 4 5 6 7 (Max)

    c) How much do you consider that your personal effort can affect the amount that you will get in the future?   (Min) 1 2 3 4 5 6 7 (Max)

    d) How important is this to you?   (Min) 1 2 3 4 5 6 7 (Max)

3 — An adequate salary.
  a) How much is there now? (Min) 1 2 3 4 5 6 7 (Max)
  b) How much would you like it to be? (Min) 1 2 3 4 5 6 7 (Max)
  c) How much do you consider that your personal effort can affect the amount that you will get in the future? (Min) 1 2 3 4 5 6 7 (Max)
  d) How important is this to you? (Min) 1 2 3 4 5 6 7 (Max)

4 — The opportunity to develop and express your own ideas.
  a) How much is there now? (Min) 1 2 3 4 5 6 7 (Max)
  b) How much would you like it to be? (Min) 1 2 3 4 5 6 7 (Max)
  c) How much do you consider that your personal effort can affect the amount that you will get in the future? (Min) 1 2 3 4 5 6 7 (Max)
  d) How important is this to you? (Min) 1 2 3 4 5 6 7 (Max)

5 — The feeling of pressure in your professoral position.
  a) How much is there now? (Min) 1 2 3 4 5 6 7 (Max)
  b) How much would you like it to be? (Min) 1 2 3 4 5 6 7 (Max)
  c) How much do you consider that your personal effort can affect the amount that you will get in the future? (Min) 1 2 3 4 5 6 7 (Max)
  d) How important is this to you? (Min) 1 2 3 4 5 6 7 (Max)

6 — The opportunity to contribute to the development of the philosophy of your university.
  a) How much is there now? (Min) 1 2 3 4 5 6 7 (Max)
  b) How much would you like it to be? (Min) 1 2 3 4 5 6 7 (Max)
  c) How much do you consider that your personal effort can affect the amount that you will get in the future? (Min) 1 2 3 4 5 6 7 (Max)
  d) How important is this to you? (Min) 1 2 3 4 5 6 7 (Max)

7 — The feeling that you can make good use of your knowledge, abilities, and capabilities in your job.

a) How much is there now?   (Min) 1 2 3 4 5 6 7 (Max)
b) How much would you like it
   to be?   (Min) 1 2 3 4 5 6 7 (Max)
c) How much do you consider that
   your personal effort can affect
   the amount that you will get in
   the future?   (Min) 1 2 3 4 5 6 7 (Max)
d) How important is this to you?   (Min) 1 2 3 4 5 6 7 (Max)

8 — The opportunity to develop close
    friendships in you position.
    a) How much is there now?   (Min) 1 2 3 4 5 6 7 (Max)
    b) How much would you like it
       to be?   (Min) 1 2 3 4 5 6 7 (Max)
    c) How much do you consider that
       your personal effort can affect
       the amount that you will get in
       the future?   (Min) 1 2 3 4 5 6 7 (Max)
    d) How important is this to you?   (Min) 1 2 3 4 5 6 7 (Max)

9 — The opportunity to get promotions.
    a) How much is there now?   (Min) 1 2 3 4 5 6 7 (Max)
    b) How much would you like it
       to be?   (Min) 1 2 3 4 5 6 7 (Max)
    c) How much do you consider that
       your personal effort can affect
       the amount that you will get in
       the future?   (Min) 1 2 3 4 5 6 7 (Max)
    d) How important is this to you?   (Min) 1 2 3 4 5 6 7 (Max)

10 — The opportunity to get recognition
     from people you respect.
     a) How much is there now?   (Min) 1 2 3 4 5 6 7 (Max)
     b) How much would you like it
        to be?   (Min) 1 2 3 4 5 6 7 (Max)
     c) How much do you consider that
        your personal effort can affect
        the amount that you will get in
        the future?   (Min) 1 2 3 4 5 6 7 (Max)
     d) How important is this to you?   (Min) 1 2 3 4 5 6 7 (Max)

Section II

Below, you will find a series of activities which professors in a university may be concerned with to a greater or lesser extent. Using the following scale, please tell: (a) How important are each of these in order for your university's to achieve its goals? (b) How important is doing it in order for you to get the rewards offered by the university?

1 — Participating in the designing of the curriculum of your department.

   a) How important is doing it for your university to achieve it goals? (Min) 1 2 3 4 5 6 7 (Max)

   b) How important is doing it in the determination of your rewards by the university? (Min) 1 2 3 4 5 6 7 (Max)

2 — Representing the faculty in the "Academic Senate" or "Administrative Board".

   a) How important is doing it for your university to achieve it goals? (Min) 1 2 3 4 5 6 7 (Max)

   b) How important is doing it in the determination of your rewards by the university? (Min) 1 2 3 4 5 6 7 (Max)

3 — Representing your university in activities in your community such as the Conferences of the Coop, Public Dates, etc.

   a) How important is doing it for your university to achieve its goals? (Min) 1 2 3 4 5 6 7 (Max)

   b) How important is doing it in the determination of your rewards by the university? (Min) 1 2 3 4 5 6 7 (Max)

4 — Working in your department's presentation in the university "Open House".

   a) How important is doing it for your university to achieve it goals? (Min) 1 2 3 4 5 6 7 (Max)

   b) How important is doing it in the determination of your rewards by the university? (Min) 1 2 3 4 5 6 7 (Max)

5 — Doing research and publishing books and articles.

   a) How important is doing it for your university to achieve it goals? (Min) 1 2 3 4 5 6 7 (Max)

   b) How important is doing it in the
determination of your rewards
by the university?   (Min) 1 2 3 4 5 6 7 (Max)

6 — Write new syllabus for your courses.

   a) How important is doing it for
your university to achieve its
goals?   (Min) 1 2 3 4 5 6 7 (Max)

   b) How important is doing it in the
determination of your rewards
by the university?   (Min) 1 2 3 4 5 6 7 (Max)

7 — Evaluating textbooks for your
courses.

   a) How important is doing it for
your university to achieve its
goals?   (Min) 1 2 3 4 5 6 7 (Max)

   b) How important is doing it in the
determination of your rewards
by the university?   (Min) 1 2 3 4 5 6 7 (Max)

8 — Receiving awards from your university or any university or organization.

   a) How important is doing it for
your university to achieve its
goals?   (Min) 1 2 3 4 5 6 7 (Max)

   b) How important is doing it in the
determination of your rewards
by the university?   (Min) 1 2 3 4 5 6 7 (Max)

9 — Teaching a course that is thought to
be interesting and well designed by
your students and co-workers.

   a) How important is doing it for
your university to achieve its
goals?   (Min) 1 2 3 4 5 6 7 (Max)

   b) How important is doing it in the
determination of your rewards
by the university?   (Min) 1 2 3 4 5 6 7 (Max)

10 — Improving your teaching methods
(using any method that you consider
useful like film, field trips, etc.).

   a) How important is doing it for
your university to achieve its
goals?   (Min) 1 2 3 4 5 6 7 (Max)

   b) How important is doing it in the
determination of your rewards
by the university?   (Min) 1 2 3 4 5 6 7 (Max)

11 — Working in the registration process of your university.

   a) How important is doing it for your university to achieve its goals?   (Min) 1 2 3 4 5 6 7 (Max)

   b) How important is doing it in the determination of your rewards by the university?   (Min) 1 2 3 4 5 6 7 (Max)

12 — Participating in the high s c h o o l orientation in order to recruit new students every year.

   a) How important is doing it for ·your university to achieve its goals?   (Min) 1 2 3 4 5 6 7 (Max)

   b) How important is doing it in the determination of your rewards by the university?   (Min) 1 2 3 4 5 6 7 (Max)

13 — Participating on committees in your university as the Library's Committee, etc.

   a) How important is doing it for your university to achieve its goals?   (Min) 1 2 3 4 5 6 7 (Max)

   b) How important is doing it in the determination of your rewards by the university?   (Min) 1 2 3 4 5 6 7 (Max)

14 — Counseling or orientation of students as to academic affairs and personal problems.

   a) How important is doing it for your university to achieve its goals?   (Min) 1 2 3 4 5 6 7 (Max)

   b) How important is doing it in the determination of your rewards by the university?   (Min) 1 2 3 4 5 6 7 (Max)

15 — Having or studying for a Ph. D. degree.

   a) How important is doing it for your university to achieve its goals?   (Min) 1 2 3 4 5 6 7 (Max)

   b) How important is doing it in the determination of your rewards by the university?   (Min) 1 2 3 4 5 6 7 (Max)

16 — Taking new courses in your field to refresh your knowledge.

    a) How important is doing it for your university to achieve its goals?   (Min) 1 2 3 4 5 6 7 (Max)

    b) How important is doing it in the determination of your rewards by the university?   (Min) 1 2 3 4 5 6 7 (Max)

Section III

Below, you will find a series of situations or working conditions that can be present in your university. Would you please answer all of these statements about working conditions in your university?

1 — There are some co-workers in administrative positions having a higher salary and better working conditions than I, even though I have more experience and better education than they.

    a) strongly agree b) agree c) undecided d) disagree e) strongly disagree

2 — I am working very hard in order to do a good job, but my university seems unaware of this.

    a) strongly agree b) agree c) undecided d) disagree e) strongly disagree

3 — In this university some professors work hard, but others often get the credit for the work done.

    a) strongly agree b) agree c) undecided d) disagree e) strongly disagree

4 — My working conditions are fair when we compare them with the working conditions of other professionals with the same level of education, experience, and responsibilities in other organizations.

    a) strongly agree b) agree c) undecided d) disagree e) strongly disagree

5 — There are some professionals with less qualifications that I having the same or better working conditions in other organizations.

    a) strongly agree b) agree c) undecided d) disagree e) strongly disagree

6 — I think that my present working conditions are fair.

    a) strongly agree b) agree c) undecided d) disagree e) strongly disagree

7 — I have the same opportunity to obtain a high administrative position as my co-workers who have qualifications similar to mine.

a) strongly agree b) agree c) undecided d) disagree e) strongly disagree

Section IV

1 — I would accept a proposal to work as professor in another university with an increase of $ 1,200 per year over my present salary.
a) strongly agree b) agree c) undecided d) disagree e) strongly disagree

2 — How often do you do some extra work for your job which is not really required of you?
a) almost every day b) several times a week c) about once a week d) once every few weeks e) about once a month or less

3 — Whenever I hear (or read about) some one criticizing my university it makes me quite angry.
a) strongly agree b) agree c) undecided d) disagree e) strongly disagree

4 — This university is making a great contribution to our national education.
a) strongly agree b) agree c) undecided d) disagree e) strongly disagree

5 — My university is a large family in which the employees feel a sense of belonging.
a) strongly agree b) agree c) undecided d) disagree e) strongly disagree

6 — The employees of this university must feel great pride in being part of it.
a) strongly agree b) agree c) undecided d) disagree e) strongly disagree

7 — How often do you participate in the extra curricular activities sponsored by your university (such as concerts, conferences, etc.)?
a) always b) very frequently c) occasionally d) rarely e) almost never

Section V

1 — How important is the opinion about the quality of your present performance of each one of the following people?

	Very Important	Important	Undecided	Slightly Important	Unimportant
A — Your students					
B — Students in general					
C — Chairman					
D — Dean					
E — Colleagues in other universities					
F — Co-workers					
G — People outside of your university					

2 — How often do you get information about their opinion about the quality of the job you are doing?

	Every Week	Every Month	One or two times in a semester	One or two times in a year	Never
A — Your students					
B — Students in general					
C — Chairman					
D — Dean					
E — Colleagues in other universities					
F — Co-workers					
G — People outside of your university					

3 — Consider your normal day at your job. Estimate the percentage of the total time you give to each of the following activities.

a) —— % Preparing your lesson for next time.
b) —— % Attending committee meetings.
c) —— % Being available to counsel students.

d) —— % Teaching.

e) —— % Studying in your specialization (doing research, reading articles, books, taking courses, etc.).

f) —— % Working in administrative affairs (filing reports, writting letters, etc.).

  100 % = Total

Section VI

1 — Tell the degree of influence that people outside your institution tend to exert in the following activities. How much do you think they should have? Use an X to tell the actual degree of influence and N to tell how much you think they should have.

	Great Deal	Some	Very Little	None
Example: Job description of janitors.			X	N
A — Faculty recruitment				
B — Student admission to your department				
C — University's budget distribution				
D — Selection of university administrators (Dean, Rector, etc.)				
E — Changing the curriculum				
F — Establishment of a new academic program				
G — Faculty's promotions, tenure, etc.				

2 — Tell the amount of participation that you personally usually have in deciding about the following activities in your university. How much do you think you should have? Use an X to tell the amount of participation that you usually have at the present time in the decision and an N to tell how much participation you think you should have.

	Great Deal	Some	Very Little	None
Example: Job description of janitors.			X	N
A — Faculty recruitment				
B — Student admission to your department				
C — University budget distribution				
D — Selection of university administrators (Rector, Dean, etc.)				
E — Changing the curriculum				
F — Establishment of a new academic program				
G — Faculty's promotions, tenure, etc.				

3 — In general a very friendly atmosphere prevails among the people working in our university.

a) strongly agree b) agree c) undecided d) disagree e) strongly disagree

4 — The attitude of all our university personnel is to work in a friendly way toward the university's goal.

a) strongly agree b) agree c) undecided d) disagree e) strongly disagree

5 — In this university the professors have complete freedom to design the courses, choose the course's text-books and determine all matters about the academic features of the courses.

a) strongly agree b) agree c) undecided d) disagree e) strongly disagree

6 — Professors have freedom to express their own opinion in the classroom.

a) strongly agree b) agree c) undecided d) disagree e) strongly disagree

7 — Excessive rules, administrative details, and red-tape make it difficult for a professor to do his job in an adequate way in this university.

a) strongly agree b) agree c) undecided d) disagree e) strongly disagree

8 — The university has always been fair giving promotions and tenure.
a) strongly agree b) agree c) undecided d) disagree e) strongly disagree

9 — The university never keeps its promises over the years about the teaching load, adequate facilities, etc.
a) strongly agree b) agree c) undecided d) disagree e) strongly disagree

10 — The recommendations of my Chairman and Dean are usually supported by the Chancellor, the President, and the Council of Higher Education.
a) strongly agree b) agree c) undecided d) disagree e) strongly disagree

11 — I think that the tenure system is necessary in my university to safeguard academic freedom.
a) strongly agree b) agree c) undecided d) disagree e) strongly disagree

12 — How much do rules and procedures guide decisions made in the following areas? Use an X to answer each one of these questions.

	Great Deal	Some	Very Little	None
A — Faculty recruitment				
B — Student admission to your department				
C — University budget distribution				
D — Selection of university administrators (Rector, Dean, etc.)				
E — Changing the curriculum				
F — Establishment of a new academic program				
G — Faculty's promotions, tenure, etc.				

13 — How free do you feel to criticize poor decisions in the following areas? Use and X to answer each one of these questions.

	Great Deal	Some	Very Little	None
A — Faculty recruitment				
B — Student admission to your department				
C — University budget distribution				
D — Selection of university administrators (Rector, Dean, etc.)				
E — Changing the curriculum				
F — Establishment of a new academic program				
G — Faculty's promotions, tenure, etc.				

Section VII

In the execution of a job two factors would have strong importance: effort and performance. *Effort* is the amount of energy an individual expends in a given situation. The concept of effort and performance are different. For example, a student might study hard in order to prepare for an exam (effort) but get a low grade (performance).

Using the scale below, rank the degree of effort that you expend in your present job.

Degree of Effort

1 — Effort that I expend in my job: (Min) 1 2 3 4 5 6 7 (Max)

Tell how you rate the quality of your performance in your university using the following scale:

Quality of your Performance

2 — My performance in the university must be rated as: (Min) 1 2 3 4 5 6 7 (Max)

3 — In general, how satisfied are you with your present position at this university (consider the overall aspects of your job)?   (Min) 1 2 3 4 5 6 7 (Max)

Section VIII

Academic Rank _____   Age _____

Employment Status _____   Annual Salary _____

Time Working at it _____   Department Name _____

Career Field _____   University _____

Education _____

*Reliability and Validity Results
of the Pilot Study*

Equity Section — First Analysis

Pearson Product — Moment Intercorrelations

Items =	117	118	119	120	121	115	116
Total R =	.394	.665	.667	.611	.567	—.135	.200

Items =	122	123
Total R =	.639	.468

Total Obverse = .803

Total Reverse = .67

Guttman analysis

   Total Errors 74.0

   Coefficient of Reproducibility = .817

Green B

   Total Error = 69.2

   Coefficient of Reproducibility = .829

Weaver Index of Consistency = .009
Loevinger Index of Homogeneity = .193
Kuder-Richardson 20 = .604
Corrected K — R 20 = .626

Analysis of Multilevel Responses

Kuder-Richardson Reliability	Inferred Ave. Inter-Item Correlation
Obverse items = .691	.358
Reverse items = .291	.07
Total items = .516	.106
Standard error of measurement = 4.0	
Standard error of estimated = 2.8	

Analysis of Single Factoredness

Degrees of freedom = 27
Probability = .0004
Sigma mean = .2735
Sigma residual = .1178
Expected sigma = .0706
Wollins Index of Single — Factoredness .7675

Equity Section — Second Analysis

Pearson Product — Moment Intercorrelations

Items =	117	118	119	120	121	122	123
Total R =	.553	.711	.703	.638	.607	.623	.443

Total Obverse = .908
Total Reverse = .773

Guttman Analysis

Total Errors = 44.0
Coefficient of Reproducibility = .860

Green B

Total Errors = 40.6
Coefficient of Reproducibility = .870

Green Index of Consistency = .387
Weaver Index of Consistency = .242
Loevinger Index of Homogeneity = .333
Kuder-Richardson 20 = .712
Kuder-Richardson Corrected = .740

Analysis of Multilevel Responses

Kuder-Richardson Reliability	Inferred Ave. Inter-Item Correlation
Obverse items = .691	= .38
Reverse items = .524	= .268
Total items = .723	= .271

Standard measurement
of errors = 3.2
Standard error of
estimate = 2.7

Analysis of Single Factoredeness

Degrees of Freedom = 14
Probability = .235
Sigma mean = .302

Sigma residual = .0737
Expected sigma = .0575
Wollins Index of Single — Factoredness .9339

Identification Section — First Analysis
Pearson Product — Moment Intercorrelations

Items =	124	125	126	127	129	130	131
Total R =	.392	.612	.366	.716	.772	.741	.744

Total Obverse = .594
Total Reverse = .933

Guttman Analysis

Total Errors = 48.0
Coefficient of Reproducibility = .867

Green B

Total Errors = 47.9
Coefficient of Reproducibility = .867

Green Index of Consistency = .319
Weaver Index of Consistency = .172
Loevinger Index of Homogeneity = .349
Kuder-Richardson 20 = .738
Corrected Kuder-Richardson = .770

Analysis of Multilevel Responses

Kuder-Richardson Reliability	Inferred Ave. Inter-Item Correlation
Obverse items = .478	= .314
Reverse items = .743	= .235
Total items = .719	= .242

Standard measurement
errors = 3.0
Standard error of
estimate = 2.5

Analysis of Single Factoredness

Degrees of Freedom = 20
Probability = .045
Sigma mean = .3579
Sigma residual = .0876
Expected sigma = .0343
Wollins Index of Single Factoredness = .8352

Academic Freedom — First Analysis
Pearson Product — Moment Intercorrelations

Items	=	183	184	185	186
Total R	=	.844	.809	.251	.176

Total Obverse =
Total Reverse = 1.0
Guttman Analysis

  Total Errors = 7.0
  Coefficient of Reproducibility = 6.1

Green B

  Total Errors = 7.0
  Coefficient of Reproducibility = .961
Green Index of Consistency = .321
Weaver Index of Consistency = .308
Loevinger Index of Homogeneity = .393
Kuder-Richardson 20 = .448
Corrected Kuder-Richardson = .597

Analysis of Multilevel Responses   Inferred Ave. Inter-
Kuder-Richardson Reliability   Item Correlation

  Obverse items = —
  Reverse items = —
  Total items = .373   .129
  Standard measurement
    errors = .19
  Standard errors of
    estimate = 1.1

Analysis of Single Factoredness

  Degrees of Freedom = 2
  Probability = .205
  Sigma mean = .254
  Sigma residual = .04
  Expected sigma = .003
  Wollins Index of Single Factoredness = .8480

Academic Freedom — Second Analysis
Pearson Product — Moment Intercorrelations

Items	=	183	184	185
Total R	=	.812	.823	.866

Total Obverse = —
Total Reverse = —
Guttman Analysis

  Total Errors = 3.2
  Coefficient of Reproducibility = 96.3

Green B

Total Errors = 3.2
Coefficient of Reproducibility = .963

Green Index of Consistency = .452
Weaver Index of Consistency = .408
Loevinger Index of Homogeneity = .432
Kuder-Richardson 20 = .686
Corrected K — R = .724

Analysis of Multilevel Responses

Kuder-Richardson Reliability	Inferred Ave. Inter-Item Correlation
Obverse items = —	
Reverse items = —	
Total items = .462	.168
Standard measurement errors = 1.0	
Standard errors estimate = 1.0	

Analysis of Single Factoredness

Degrees of Freedom = 2
Probability = .205
Sigma mean = .206
Sigma residual = .04
Expected sigma = .003
Wollins Index of Single Factoredness = .864

Trust Section — First Analysis

Items =	189	190	191	192
Total R =	.230	.325	.496	.666

Total Obverse = 1.0
Total Reverse = —
Guttman Analysis

Total Errors = 13.0
Coefficient of Reproducibility = .928

Green B

Total Errors = 13.1
Coefficient of Reproducibility = .927

Green Index of Consistency = —.246
Weaver Index of Consistency = —.167

Loevinger Index of Homogeneity = —.246
Kuder-Richardson 20 = —.494
Corrected K — R = —.708

Analysis of Multilevel Responses

Kuder-Richardson Realiability	Inferred Ave. Inter-Item Correlation
Obverse items = .07	
Reverse items = .07	—.073
Total items = .07	
Standard measurement errors = 2.6	
Standard Error estimate = —	

Analysis of Single Factoredness

Degrees of Freedom = 2
Probability = .0000
Sigma mean = .2153
Sigma residual = .1362
Expected sigma = .009
Wollins Index of Single Factoredness = .3850

*Reliability and Validity Results
of the Final Study*

Trust Section — First Analysis
Pearson Product — Moment Intercorrelations

Items =	140	141	142	143
Total R =	.541	.454	.644	.559

Total Obverse = .758
Total Reverse = .747
Guttman Analysis

Total Errors = 120.0
Coefficient of Reproducibility = .911

Green B

Total Errors = 121.2
Coefficient of Reproducibility = .910

Green Index of Consistency = .201
Weaver Index of Consistency = .186
Loevinger Index of Homogeneity = .206
Kuder-Richardson 20 = .342
Corrected K — R = .410

Analysis of Multilevel Responses

	Inferred Ave. Inter-Item Correlation
Kuder-Richardson Reliability	
Obverse items = .105	.056
Reverse items = .454	.293
Total items = .319	.105
Standard measurement errors = 2.2	
Standard errors estimate = 1.4	

Analysis of Single Factoredness

      Degrees of Freedom = 2
      Probability = .331
      Sigma mean = .1601
      Sigma residual = .0208
      Expected sigma = .016
      Wollins Index of Single Factoredness = .9669

Equity Section — First Analysis
Pearson Product — Moment Intercorrelations

Items =	73	74	75	76	77	78	79
Total R =	.356	.402	.137	.030	.171	.325	.571

Total Obverse = .530
Total Reverse = .610
Guttman Analysis

      Total Errors = 248.0
      Coefficient of Reproducibility = .823

Green B

      Total Errors = 224.9
      Coefficient of Reproducibility = .839

Green Index of Consistency = .071
Weaver Index of Consistency = .092
Loevinger Index of Homogeneity = .071
Kuder-Richardson 20 = —.439
Corrected K — R = —.475

Analysis of Multilevel Responses

Kuder Richardson Reliability	Inferred Ave. Inter-Item Correlation
Obverse items = —.137	—.0
Reverse items = —.249	—.052
Total items = —.878	—.072

      Standard measurement
        errors = 3.3
      Standard estimate
        of errors = —

Analysis of Single Factoredness

      Degrees of Freedom = 14
      Probability = .0000
      Sigma means = .29
      Sigma residual = .2096

Expected sigma = .0113
Wollins Index of Single Factoredness = .3081

Equity — Second Analysis
Pearson Product — Moment Intercorrelations

Items =	73	74	78	79
Total R =	.476	.580	.462	.721

Total Obverse = .718
Total Reverse = .860

Guttman Analysis

Total Errors = 226.0
Coefficient of Reproducibility = .962

Green B

Total Errors = 221.7
Coefficient of Reproducibility = .962

Green Index of Consistency = .426
Loevinger Index of Homogeneity = .386
Kuder-Richardson 20 = .262
Corrected Kuder-Richardson = .312

Analysis of Multilevel Responses

Kuder-Richardson Reliability	Inferred Ave. Inter-Item Correlation
Obverse items = .190	.107
Reverse items = .628	.363
Total items = .486	.286

Standard measurement
errors = 3.2

Analysis of Single Factoredness

Degrees of Freedom = 14
Probability = .0000
Sigma mean = 2600
Sigma residual = .0406
Expected sigma = .0208
Wollins Index of Single Factoredness = .864

Identification Section — First Analysis
Pearson Product — Moment Intercorrelation

Items =	80	81	82	83	84	85	86
Total R =	.267	.161	1661	.750	.666	.751	.344

Total Revers = .951

Total Obverse = .267
Guttman Analysis
    Total Errors = 416.0
    Coefficient of Reproducibility = .824

Green B
    Total Errors = 396.0
    Coefficient of Reproducibility = .833
Green Index of Consistency = .136
Weaver Index of Consistency = .035
Loevinger Index of Homogencity = .144
Kuder-Richardson 20 = .446
Corrected K — R = .472

Analysis of Multilevel Responses

Kuder-Richardson Reliability	Inferred Ave. Inter-Item Correlation
Obverse items =	
Reverse items =	
Total items = .534	.141
Standard measurement of errors = 3.0	

Analysis of Single Factoredness
    Degrees of freedom = 14
    Probability = .0000
    Sigma mean = .2853
    Sigma residual = .0505
    Expected sigma = .017
    Wollins Index of Single Factoredness = .876

Academic Freedom — First Analysis
Pearson Product — Moment Intercorrelations
    Items = 137 138
    Total R = .873 .833
Guttman Analysis
    Total Errors = 21.0
    Coefficient of Reproducibility = .969

Green B
    Total Errors = 21.0
    Coefficient of Reproducibility = .969
Green Index of Consistency = .590

Weaver Index of Consistency = .590
Loevinger Index of Homogeneity = .590
Kuder and Richardson 20 = .579
Corrected K — R = .709

Analysis of Multilevel Responses

	Inferred Ave. Inter-Item Correlation
Kuder-Richardson Reliability	
Total items = .624	.453

The Single Factoredness analysis is not computed when the scale has less than four items.

Results:
Role Perception — First Analysis
Pearson Product — Moment Intercorrelations

Items =	41	43	45	47	49	51	53
Total R =	.482	.302	.376	.464	.325	.498	.521
Items =	55	57	59	61	63	65	67
Total R =	.462	.333	.298	.356	.416	.397	.368
Items =	69	71					
Total R =	.423	.456					

Guttman Analysis

Total Errors = 476.0
Coefficient of Reproducibility = .846

Green B

Total Errors = 489.0
Coefficient of Reproducibility = .824

Green Index of Consistency = .268
Weaver Index of Consistency = .218
Loevinger Index of Homogeneity = .390
Kuder-Richardson 20 = .478
Kuder-Richardson Corrected = .518

Analysis of Multilevel Responses

	Inferred Ave. Inter-Item Correlation
Kuder-Richardson Reliability	
Total = .482	= .189

Analysis of Single Factoredness

Degrees of Freedom = 32
Probability = .0000
Sigma mean = .486
Sigma residual = .0506
Expected sigma = .0203
Wollins Index of Single Factoredness = .826

BIBLIOGRAPHY

Alderfer, Clayton P., *Existence, Relatedness, and Growth: Human Needs in Organizational Settings*, New York, N. Y., The Free Press, 1972.

Alutto, Joseph and Belasco, James, "A Typology for Participation in Organizational Decision Making," *Administrative Science Quarterly*, 1972, *17*, 117-125.

Atkinson, J. W., *An Introduction to Motivation*, Princeton, N. J., Van Nostrand, 1964.

Bennis, W. G. *et al.*, "The Nature of Profession," in Nelson B. Henry (ed.), *Education for the Professions*, Chicago, Ill., University of Chicago Press, 1962.

Berlew, D. and Hall, D. T. "The Socialization of Managers: Effects of Expectation on Performance," *Administrative Science Quarterly*, 1966, *2*, 207-223.

Blume, S. and Sinclair, R., "Chemist in British Universities: A Study of the Reward System in Science," *American Sociological Review*, 1967, *32*, 391-407.

Brayfield, A. and Crockett, W., "Employee Attitudes and Employee Performance," *Psychological Bulletin*, 1955, *55*, 396-424.

Burns, John A., "A Manual to Accompany Program ATSCALE: Evaluation of the Unidimensionality and Internal Consistency of Responses to a Series of Questions," Department of Psychology, Northwestern University, Evanston, Illinois, 1974.

Campbell, John P. *et al.*, *Managerial Behavior, Performance, and Effectiveness*, New York, N. Y., McGraw-Hill Book Co., 1970.

Caplow, T. and McGree, R. J., *The Academic Market Place*, New York, N. Y., Basic Books, 1958.

Deci, Edward, "The Effects of Contingent and Non-contingent Rewards and Controls of Intrinsic Motivation," *Organization Behavior and Human Performance*, 1972, *8*, 217-229.

DeVries, David L., "The Relationship of Role Expectations to Faculty Behavior," Center for Social Organization of Schools, The John Hopkins University, Baltimore, Maryland, Technical Report, 1972.

Duncan, Robert, "Characteristics of Organizational Environments and Perceived Environmental Uncertainty," *Administrative Science Quarterly*, 1972, *17*, 313-327.

Eble, Kenneth E., *Professors as Teachers*, San Francisco, Calif., Jossey Bass, Inc., 1972.

Eckert, R. E. and Anderson, D., *The University of Minnesota Faculty: Who Serves and Why?*, Minneapolis, Minn., University of Minnesota, 1970.

Eckert, R. E. and Stecklein, J. E., *Job Motivation and Satisfactions of College Teachers*, Cooperative Research Monograph, No. 7, U. S. Government Printing Office, 1961.

Etzioni, Amitai, *Modern Organizations*, Englewood Cliffs, N. J., Prentice Hall, 1964.

Evans, Martin G., "The Effects of Supervisory Behavior on the Path-Goal Relationship," *Journal of Organizational Behavior and Human Performance*, 1970, *5*, 277-298.

Galbraith, Jay Robert, *Motivational Determinants of Job Performance*. Unpublished doctoral dissertation, Indiana University, 1966.

Georopoulos, Basil, "Individual Performance and Job Satisfaction Differences Explained with Instrumentality Theory and Expectancy Models as a Function of Path-Goal Relationships." Reprinted from *Progress and Clinical Psychology*, New York, N. Y., Orune & Stratton, Inc., 1971.

———— et al., "A Path-Goal Approach to Productivity," *Journal of Applied Psychology*, 1957, *41*, 345-353.

Gibb, J. R., Defensive Communication," in D. Kolb *et al.* (eds.), *Organizational Psychology*, Englewood Cliffs, N. J., Prentice Hall, 1974.

Glaser, Barney, "The Local-Cosmopolitan Scientist," *American Journal of Sociology*, 1963, *69*, 249-259.

Gouldner, Alvin, *Patterns of Industrial Bureaucracy*, Glencoe, Ill., Free Press, 1954.

Graen, George, "Instrumentality Theory of Work Motivation: Some Experimental Results in Suggested Modifications," *Journal of Applied Psychology*, 1969, *53*, 1-15.

Greene, Charles N., "Causal Connections Among Managers' Merit Pay, Job Satisfaction, and Performance," *Journal of Applied Psychology*, 1973, *58*, 95-100.

Hall, Douglas T. and Lawler, Edward, "Job Characteristics and Pressures and the Organizational Integration of Professionals," *Administrative Science Quarterly*, 1970, *15*, 271-281.

Hall, Douglas T. *et al.*, "Personal Factors in Organizational Identification," *Administrative Science Quarterly*, 1970, *15*, 176-190.

Hangstrom, W., *The Scientific Community*, New York, N. Y., Basic Books, 1965.

Herzberg, Frederick *et al.*, *The Motivation to Work*, New York, N. Y., John Wiley & Son, Inc., 1959.

House, Robert and Rizzo, John, "Role Conflict and Ambiguity as Critical Variables in a Model of Organizational Behavior," *Organizational Behavior and Human Performance*, 1972, *7*, 467-505.

Inkson, J. H. *et al.*, "Extending the Occupational Environment," *Journal of Occupational Psychology*, 1972, *41*, 33-47.

Juralewicz, R. S., "Interpersonal Dimensions of Decision Making in a Cross-Cultural Setting," Graduate School of Business, University of Puerto Rico, 1972.

Kahn, Robert *et al.*, *Organizational Stress: Studies in Role Conflict and Ambiguity*, New York, N. Y., John Wiley & Son, Inc., 1964, pp. 71-94.

Kavcic, Bogdan *et al.*, "Control, Participation, and Effectiveness in Four Yugoslav Industrial Organizations," *Administrative Science Quarterly*, 1971, 16, 74-87.

Lawler, Edward, *Pay and Organizational Effectiveness: A Psychological View*, New York, N. Y., McGraw-Hill Co., 1971.

————. *Motivation in Work Organizations*, Alton, California, Brooks/Cole Publishing Company, 1973.

Lichtman, Cary and Hunt, Raymond, "Personality and Organization Theory: A Review of Some Conceptual Literature," *Psychological Bulletin*, 1971, 76, 271-294.

Litwin, G. and Stringer, R., *Motivation and Organizational Climate*, Boston, Mass., Harvard University, Graduate School of Business Administration, 1968.

Lyons, Thomas, "Role Clarity, Need for Clarity, Satisfaction, Tension, and Withdrawal," *Organizational Behavior and Human Performance*, 1971, *6*, 99-110.

Maslow, Abraham, "A Theory of Human Motivation," *Psychological Review*, 1943, *50*, 370-396.

————, *Motivation and Personality*, New York, N. Y., Harper, 1954.

Mayo, E. *The Human Problems of an Industrial Civilization*, New York, N. Y., MacMillan Co., 1933.

McCarrey, Michael and Edwards, Shirley, "Organizational Climate Conditions for Effective Research Scientist Role Performance," *Organization Behavior and Human Performance*, 1973, *9*, 439-459.

McGregor, Douglas, *The Human Side of Enterprise*, New York, N. Y., McGraw-Hill Book Co., 1960.

Mitchell, T. and Albright, D., "Expectancy Theory Predictions of the Satisfaction, Effort, Performance and Retention of Naval Aviation Offices," *Organizational Behavior and Human Performance*, 1972, *8*, 1-20.

Mitchell, T. and Nebeker, D., "Expectancy Theory Predictions of Academic Effort and Performance," *Journal of Applied Psychology*, 1973, *57*, 6-67.

Mitchell, T. and Pollard, W., "Effort, Ability, and Role Perception as Predictor of Job Performance," Seattle, Washington, University of Washington, 1973.

Nisbet, R., *The Degradation of the Academic Dogma: The University of America, 1945-70*, New York, N. Y., Basic Books, 1971.

Parsons, Talcott, "Suggestions for a Sociological Approach to the Theory of Organizations, II," *Administrative Science Quarterly*, 1956, *1*, 225-239.

Patchen, Martin, *Participation, Achievement and Involvement on the Job*, Englewood Cliffs, N. J., Prentice Hall, 1970.

Peak, H., "Attitude and Motivation," in M. R. Jones (ed.), *Nebraska Symposium on Motivation*, Lincoln, Nebr., University of Nebraska Press, 1955.

Porter, Lyman, "A Study of Perceived Need Satisfaction in Bottom and Middle Management Jobs," *Journal of Applied Psychology*, 1961, *45*, 1-10.

————— and Lawler E., *Managerial Attitudes and Performance*, Homewood, Illinois, Richard D. Irwin Publishing Co., 1968.

Pritchard, Robert D. and De Leo, Phillip, "Experimental Test of the Valence—Instrumentality Relationship in Job Performance," *Journal of Applied Psychology*, 1973, *51*, 264-270.

Pritchard, R. and Sanders, M., "The Influence of Valence, Instrumentality, and Expectancy on Effort and Performance," *Journal of Applied Psychology*, 1973, *57*, 55-60.

Pritchard, Robert D. *et al.*, "Effects of Perception of Equity and Inequity on Worker Performance and Satisfaction," *Journal of Applied Psychology*, 1972, *56*, 75-94.

Raven, Bertram H., "Social Influence and Power," in I. D. Steiner and M. Fishbein (eds.), *Current Studies in Social Psychology*, New York, N. Y., Holt, Rinehart, and Winston, 1965.

Rizzo, John R. *et al.*, "Role Conflict and Ambiguity in Complex Organizations," *Administrative Science Quarterly*, 1970, *15*, 150-163.

Schein, E. H., *Organizational Psychology*, Englewood Cliffs, N. J. Prentice Hall, 1965.

Schuster, Jay R. *et al.*, "Testing Portions of Porter and Lawler Model Regarding the Motivational Role of Pay," *Journal of Applied Psychology*, 1971, *55*, 187-195.

Scott, Wm. G. and Mitchell, T., *Organization Theory: A Structural and Behavioral Analysis*, Homewood, Illinois, Irwin-Dorsey Co., 1972.

Siegel, Alan and Ruh, Robert, "Job Involvement, Participation in Decision Making, Personal Background, and Job Behavior," *Organizational Behavior and Human Performance*, 1973, *9*, 318-327.

Smith, B. L., *The Tenure Debate*, San Francisco, Calf., Jossey Bass, Inc., 1973.

Stinchcombe, Arthur L., *Constructing Social Theories*, Chicago, Ill., Harcourt, Brace and World, Inc., 1968.

Stryker, P., "On the Meaning of Executive Qualities," *Fortune*, 1958, *57*, 116-119.

Telly, Charles S. *et al.*, "The Relationship of Inequity to Turnover Among Hourly Workers," *Administrative Science Quarterly*, 1971, *16*, 164-172.

Thornton, Russell, "Organizational Involvement and Commitment to Organization and Profession," *Administrative Science Quarterly*, 1970, *15*, 417-427.

Tolman, E., "Principles of Purposive Behavior," in S. Koch (ed.), *Psychology: A Study of Science*, vol. 12, New York, N. Y., McGraw-Hill, 1959.

Tosi, Henry, "Organizational Stress as a Moderator of the Relationship Between Influence and Role Response," *Academy of Management Journal*, 1971, *14*, 47-58.

Turney, John R., "Activity Outcome Expectancies and Intrinsic Activity Values as Predictors of Several Motivation Indexes for Technical-Professionals," *Organizational Behavior and Human Performance*, 1974, *11*, 65-82.

Vroom, Victor, *Work and Motivation*, New York, N. Y., John Wiley and Son, Inc., 1964.

Wall, James Jr. and Adams, J. "Some Variables Affecting a Constituent's Evaluations of Behavior Toward a Boundary Role Occupant," *Organization Behavior and Human Performance*, 1974, *11*, 390-408.

Walton, R. E., and Mackersie, R. B., *A Behavior Theory of Labor Negotiations*, New York, N. Y., McGraw-Hill Book Co., 1965.

Zand, D. E., "Trust and Managerial Problem Solving," *Administrative Science Quarterly*, 1972, *17*, 229-239.

Este libro se terminó de imprimir
el día 1 de diciembre de 1981, en los
Talleres Gráficos de Manuel Pareja
Montaña, 16 - Barcelona - España